Child Abuse

Other Books of Related Interest:

Opposing Viewpoints Series

Conflict Resolution

Domestic Violence

Family

At Issue Series

Child Pornography

Contemporary Issues Companion

Teens and Sex

Current Controversies Series

Family Violence

"Congress shall make no law . . . abridging the freedom of speech, or of the press."

First Amendment to the U.S. Constitution

The basic foundation of our democracy is the First Amendment guarantee of freedom of expression. The Opposing Viewpoints Series is dedicated to the concept of this basic freedom and the idea that it is more important to practice it than to enshrine it.

OPPOSING
VIEWPOINTS®
SERIES

Child Abuse

Heidi Williams, Book Editor

GREENHAVEN PRESS
A part of Gale, Cengage Learning

GALE
CENGAGE Learning™

Detroit • New York • San Francisco • New Haven, Conn • Waterville, Maine • London

Christine Nasso, *Publisher*
Elizabeth Des Chenes, *Managing Editor*

© 2009 Greenhaven Press, a part of Gale, Cengage Learning.

Gale and Greenhaven Press are registered trademarks used herein under license.

For more information, contact:
Greenhaven Press
27500 Drake Rd.
Farmington Hills, MI 48331-3535
Or you can visit our Internet site at gale.cengage.com

For product information and technology assistance, contact us at

Gale Customer Support, 1-800-877-4253
For permission to use material from this text or product, submit all requests online at
www.cengage.com/permissions

Further permissions questions can be emailed to permissionrequest@cengage.com

Articles in Greenhaven Press anthologies are often edited for length to meet page require-ments. In addition, original titles of these works are changed to clearly present the main thesis and to explicitly indicate the author's opinion. Every effort is made to ensure that Greenhaven Press accurately reflects the original intent of the authors. Every effort has been made to trace the owners of copyrighted material.

Cover photograph reproduced by permission of David De Lossy/Photodisc/Getty Images.

LIBRARY OF CONGRESS CATALOGING-IN-PUBLICATION DATA

Child abuse / Heidi Williams, book editor.
p. cm. -- (Opposing viewpoints)
Includes bibliographical references and index.
ISBN-13: 978-0-7377-4354-8 (hardcover)
ISBN-13: 978-0-7377-4353-1 (pbk.)
1. Child abuse. 2. Child abuse--Prevention. 3. Child abuse--Religious aspects. I. Williams, Heidi.
HV6626.5.C4716 2009
362.76--dc22
2008049406

Printed in Mexico
3 4 5 6 7 13 12 11 10

Contents

31/16

Chapter 3: How Does Child Abuse Affect Its Victims?

Why Consider
Opposing Viewpoints?

> *"The only way in which a human being can make some approach to knowing the whole of a subject is by hearing what can be said about it by persons of every variety of opinion and studying all modes in which it can be looked at by every character of mind. No wise man ever acquired his wisdom in any mode but this."*
>
> *John Stuart Mill*

In our media-intensive culture it is not difficult to find differing opinions. Thousands of newspapers and magazines and dozens of radio and television talk shows resound with differing points of view. The difficulty lies in deciding which opinion to agree with and which "experts" seem the most credible. The more inundated we become with differing opinions and claims, the more essential it is to hone critical reading and thinking skills to evaluate these ideas. Opposing Viewpoints books address this problem directly by presenting stimulating debates that can be used to enhance and teach these skills. The varied opinions contained in each book examine many different aspects of a single issue. While examining these conveniently edited opposing views, readers can develop critical thinking skills such as the ability to compare and contrast authors' credibility, facts, argumentation styles, use of persuasive techniques, and other stylistic tools. In short, the Opposing Viewpoints Series is an ideal way to attain the higher-level thinking and reading skills so essential in a culture of diverse and contradictory opinions.

In addition to providing a tool for critical thinking, Opposing Viewpoints books challenge readers to question their own strongly held opinions and assumptions. Most people form their opinions on the basis of upbringing, peer pressure, and personal, cultural, or professional bias. By reading carefully balanced opposing views, readers must directly confront new ideas as well as the opinions of those with whom they disagree. This is not to simplistically argue that everyone who reads opposing views will—or should—change his or her opinion. Instead, the series enhances readers' understanding of their own views by encouraging confrontation with opposing ideas. Careful examination of others' views can lead to the readers' understanding of the logical inconsistencies in their own opinions, perspective on why they hold an opinion, and the consideration of the possibility that their opinion requires further evaluation.

Evaluating Other Opinions

To ensure that this type of examination occurs, Opposing Viewpoints books present all types of opinions. Prominent spokespeople on different sides of each issue as well as well-known professionals from many disciplines challenge the reader. An additional goal of the series is to provide a forum for other, less known, or even unpopular viewpoints. The opinion of an ordinary person who has had to make the decision to cut off life support from a terminally ill relative, for example, may be just as valuable and provide just as much insight as a medical ethicist's professional opinion. The editors have two additional purposes in including these less known views. One, the editors encourage readers to respect others' opinions—even when not enhanced by professional credibility. It is only by reading or listening to and objectively evaluating others' ideas that one can determine whether they are worthy of consideration. Two, the inclusion of such viewpoints encourages the important critical thinking skill of objectively evaluating an author's credentials and bias. This evaluation will illuminate an author's reasons for taking a particular stance on an issue and will aid in readers' evaluation of the author's ideas.

It is our hope that these books will give readers a deeper understanding of the issues debated and an appreciation of the complexity of even seemingly simple issues when good and honest people disagree. This awareness is particularly important in a democratic society such as ours in which people enter into public debate to determine the common good. Those with whom one disagrees should not be regarded as enemies but rather as people whose views deserve careful examination and may shed light on one's own.

Thomas Jefferson once said that "difference of opinion leads to inquiry, and inquiry to truth." Jefferson, a broadly educated man, argued that "if a nation expects to be ignorant and free . . . it expects what never was and never will be." As individuals and as a nation, it is imperative that we consider the opinions of others and examine them with skill and discernment. The Opposing Viewpoints Series is intended to help readers achieve this goal.

David L. Bender and Bruno Leone,
Founders

Introduction

"The parent's right to be around his or her child is sacred in the courts. And the whole 'crying wolf' thing is hurting people."

—Rachel Feldheim,
a staff attorney at the
American Bar Association's Center
on Children and the Law.

One of the primary topics of contention in the issue of child abuse is that of parental rights. In the case of the state vs. the parent, when should the state intervene? At what point is it proper for the courts to suspend the rights of the parent and give custody of the child to the state? Also, increasingly the rights of the parent vs. the rights of the child are being considered. Do children have individual rights that supersede the rights of their parents to make decisions for them, such as the right to attend the school of their choice or the right to not go to church? Perhaps even more complex and most bitter is conflict between parents. Parents fighting over whom should have custody of a child can turn into child abuse itself and has begun receiving more attention from the courts and from children's advocates.

Parental Alienation Syndrome (PAS), a term coined by psychiatrist Richard A. Gardner in 1985, describes the manipulative power that a parent can have over their children to sabotage or poison their relationship with the other parent. In such cases, a parent might constantly criticize the other parent and make fun of the children for wanting to spend time with the other parent. Sometimes a parent will set impossible standards that the children must meet to spend time with the other parent. Or sometimes a parent simply refuses to allow the other parent any kind of contact with the children, even moving across the country to make visits more difficult.

Cathy Mannis asked her husband to leave their home after she discovered that he was having another affair. He filed for divorce and Cathy received primary custody of their three sons, but she was forced to leave them for an extended period of time because of a serious illness and her inability to support them. He promised to return them when she could manage caring for them, but instead he turned them against Cathy, moved more than a thousand miles away, warned her not to call them at all, sued for custody, and won. After several years, Cathy is still attempting to build some kind of relationship with two of her three sons. This is just one example of PAS destroying parent-child relationships.

On the other hand, because the courts are becoming more aware of the behaviors of parents who exhibit signs of PAS, attempting to alienate a child from a parent can backfire. Having been raised by her mother and stepfather from birth, after their divorce, Stephanie McDonald stayed with her stepfather every other weekend. At age 8, she started feeling uncomfortable, even panicky about the visits, and by age 10 she started to remember years of being sexually abused by her stepfather. Her stepfather denied the abuse and claimed that Stephanie's mother had planted these ideas in Stephanie's head in order to stop the visits. In light of her memories, petitions were filed to stop her stepfather's visitation rights or change them to supervised visitation. Instead, her stepfather eventually was awarded full custody of Stephanie. The judge, citing PAS, stated that her mother was manipulative and that it was better for Stephanie to live away from her.

What if Stephanie's memories were true, however, and her mother was merely reacting as any responsible mother would to protect her child? Some experts question the validity of PAS, recognizing that even if a mother behaves in a hysterical manner and is somewhat manipulative—it does not mean that abuse by the father did not occur. In fact, some experts say that PAS is used more than any other defense by fathers accused of child abuse, and there are dozens of true cases of abuse for every false accusation. Child advocates explain that because evidence often is unavailable and there may be no way to prove whether a child's memories or a parent's accusations are true, courts are forced to rule in favor of the accused parent. Furthermore, the American Psychological Association has refused a petition to classify PAS as an actual psychiatric disorder.

On the other hand one study states that 61 percent of all child abuse claims are false allegations. And anecdotal evidence seems to indicate that false claims do exist. At one school for special needs children, more than half of the staff was accused of abuse. Many were suspended and were not allowed to be alone with minors, even their own children. Yet, after months of investigation and hours in court, only one minor charge stood. In another case, Marsha Kleinman, a forensic psychologist with twenty years experience as an expert witness on child abuse, faced charges that she coached a three-year-old girl to accuse her father of molestation. Part of the evidence against Kleinman was that she did not release to the judge some facts that indicated that the toddler's statements were untrue. (For example the child said that her father's penis was green.)

Sorting out the truth is certainly difficult and in some cases even impossible. Especially in cases involving repressed memories, the child—nevermind the judge, social worker, therapist, or the parent supporting the child making the accusations—may not know the truth with absolute certainty. Research shows that even if a parent is not consciously trying to undermine another parent, speaking negatively about the other parent can damage the child's relationship with the other parent. Such parental behavior also can confuse and distress the child who loves both parents, leaving the child with emotional scars, including the inability to trust themselves and others.

Parental Alienation Syndrome remains a subject of debate. In *Opposing Viewpoints: Child Abuse* other controversies surrounding the issue of child abuse are debated in the following chapters: What Constitutes Child Abuse? What Causes Child Abuse? How Does Child Abuse Affect Its Victims? How Can Child Abuse Be Prevented? While the authors may not agree on what causes child abuse, how to stop it, or even what it is or isn't, they all strive to bring attention to this important issue.

CHAPTER 1

What Constitutes Child Abuse?

Chapter Preface

A forty-nine-year-old man pleads guilty to charges of the rape of a fifteen-year-old girl and is sentenced to thirteen months in prison. While being interviewed as a suspect in this crime, the man claimed, "I [have the right] to touch her body." When asked if he knew that it was illegal to have sex with a fifteen-year-old girl, he said "Yes, I know it's called carnal knowledge. But it's . . . custom, my culture. She is my promised wife."

Halfway around the world, a sixteen-year-old girl calls a family violence shelter asking for help. When she was fifteen years old, she was forced to marry a forty-nine-year-old man who had six other wives. She now thinks that she is pregnant, and she is afraid of her husband, who beats her and does not allow her to leave their home except for medical care. The girl is never identified, but the phone call precipitates a large investigation that subsequently leads to the removal of hundreds of children from their homes. The girl's church claims that the state is practicing religious persecution.

What is the difference between these two cases? In the first case, the man is an Aboriginal Australian. In the second case, the man is an American Fundamentalist Mormon. In both cases, however, the men live in a world outside of mainstream culture. They seem sincerely to believe that they are operating within their rights as passed down by their cultural traditions or religion.

Should modern perceptions of individual human rights take precedence over someone's religious and traditional beliefs? One view is that culture is relative—in other words, it is not right for outsiders to pass moral judgment on another culture or even another family. Religious rights trump government rights. Parents know what is right for their children and parental rights should not be overridden.

Another view is that children have individual human rights that supersede the opinions of their parents and, where applicable, religious communities. Further, it is the responsibility of the government to make sure the rights of the children are upheld.

Controversy continues over who should have the ultimate authority when it comes to deciding what is right for a child. Should outsiders, as in the local, state, or federal government or even a United Nations charter determine the definition of child abuse? Or should the views of the cultural community, such as a nuclear family or a traditional or religious community, take precedence? The following chapter discusses what constitutes child abuse and who has the right to define it.

> "Not long ago . . . various forms of spou-
> sal abuse were considered to be 'ordi-
> nary or normal.'"

Spanking Should Be Illegal

Kerby Alvy

A proposed bill in California to ban corporal punishment of children sparked a debate over the efficacy and morality of spanking and other forms of corporal punishment. The author of this viewpoint, Kerby Alvy, advocates for the proposed ban, listing harmful effects of corporal punishment, suggesting alternatives to corporal punishment, and asking the reader to consider what the existence of this debate says about how our society values children. Kerby Alvy, a clinical child psychologist, founded and directs the Center for the Improvement of Child Caring in California and is a founding board member of the National Effective Parenting Initiative.

As you read, consider the following questions:

1. What points does the author make to counter the argument that a ban on corporal punishment is not necessary because "abusive" corporal punishment is already illegal?

Kerby Alvy, "Banning Corporal Punishment: What the Arguments Tell Us about Our Character Regarding the Treatment of Children," Center for the Improvement of Child Caring, February 22, 2007. Reproduced by permission.

2. What negative outcomes do some researchers associate with parental use of corporal punishment?

3. According to the author, what does the debate over the legality of corporal punishment say about our character and how we value our children?

An impassioned debate has been raging over the airways and on editorial pages the last few weeks regarding what is permissible and effective in raising children. This has been occasioned by California Assemblywoman Sally Lieber's announcement that she will introduce legislation to ban the use of corporal punishment with children less than four years of age.

This pioneering legislation was introduced today [February 22, 2007], and the debate is likely to become even more heated.

What Is Corporal Punishment?

Corporal punishment includes a wide range of physical actions to inflict pain and discomfort, including pinching, pulling ears and hair, shaking, slapping, smacking, spanking, swatting, hitting, kicking, punching, paddling, using switches, hair brushes, belts and ironing cords, and having children kneel on gravel or a grate. The use of these punishing actions varies in intensity, harshness and length, and whether they produce crying and screaming. They also vary in regard to how often they are applied, from once or twice a year, to monthly, weekly and hourly.

These methods are used for such purposes as stopping a child's unwanted behavior, preventing the recurrence of an unwanted behavior, or because the child failed to do something the child was supposed to do. National surveys show that the majority of parents in the United States still use some of these methods, and especially with children under eight years of age. This includes 35% who admit using one or more such practices with one-year-old babies.

Most news and talk show presentations about the proposed ban focus on the more tepid forms of corporal punishment, such as spanking or swatting. They often pose the issues using both impish humor, as if this isn't serious business to the recipients of such treatment.

Newspaper editorials also focus mainly on spanking, with such clever and eye-catching headlines as, "To Spank or Not To Spank?" (*USA Today*) or "No Need for a Swat Team: Legally Banning Parents from Spanking their Children is Silly" (*Los Angeles Times*).

Those Opposing the Proposed Ban

Opponents of the proposed ban make a distinction between "ordinary or normal" corporal punishment, which is said to be mild, infrequent and does not leave physical signs like bruises, versus "abusive" corporal punishment, which leaves bruises, welts, scars, broken bones, fractured skulls and/or damaged brains. These ban opponents are loud and clear that they are opposed to the "abusive" forms, and also indicate that government has already intervened with laws banning such types of treatment.

They also seem to forget that it was not long ago that various forms of spousal abuse were considered to be "ordinary or normal" corporal punishment for women who failed to do what they were supposed to do.

These ban opponents tend to overlook the fact that "abusive" corporal punishment often begins as an instance of "ordinary" physical discipline that escalates, becomes harsher, and gets out of control, i.e., "ordinary and normal" corporal punishment is often the necessary prelude to legally defined physical abuse. Also they are hard pressed to define the point at which the "ordinary" becomes "abusive" and where the current law should come into play.

The arguments of many of the opponents of the ban are influenced by an interpretation of biblical scriptures where corporal punishment is regarded as a necessary practice if the parents' goal is to instill in children respect for authority. In addition, these opponents believe that refraining from the use of spanking and other physical force methods will have detrimental consequences such as uncontrolled, disrespectful behavior in the child. Many of these opponents are believers of the discipline methods advocated by Dr. James Dobson. In his book, *The New Dare to Discipline*, he indicates that "a small amount of discomfort goes a long way toward softening a child's rebellious spirit. However, the spanking should be of sufficient magnitude to cause genuine tears."

Those in Favor of the Proposed Ban

Those in favor of the ban draw attention to various research studies that indicate that many negative behaviors and outcomes have been regularly associated with the parental use of corporal punishment. These include greater depression, aggression and suicidal thoughts for children who are more frequent recipients of corporal punishment and of harsh corporal punishment, as well as poorer school performance and more anti-social behavior on the part of these frequently and harshly punished young people. Also, such youngsters have a higher likelihood of being victims of legally determined child abuse, probably because of the escalation effect mentioned above. These young people are also more likely to abuse their children and spouses when they grow up.

However, there is also research that suggests that these dramatic problems and outcomes are not always associated with the "ordinary, normal" applications of corporal punishment, and in some circumstances and with some cultural groups, their use is associated with positive child behaviors and outcomes. These research findings have been summarized in an August 2006 special edition of the *Cross-Cultural Research: The Journal of Comparative Social Science*. These find-

Corporal Punishment of Children in the Family

These nations have abolished corporal punishment of children in the family:

Country	Law Enacted for Families
Sweden	1979
Finland	1983
Denmark	1997
Norway	1987
Austria	1989
Cyprus	1994
Croatia	1999
Latvia	1998
Israel	1999
Germany	2000
Bulgaria	2000
Iceland	2003
Romania	2004
Ukraine	2004
Hungary	2004
Greece	2006
Netherlands	2007
New Zealand	2007
Portugal	2007
Uruguay	2007
Venezuela	2007
Spain	2007
Chile	2007

TAKEN FROM: "Discipline and the Law," *www.stophitting.com.*

ings are also reasons why some highly respected child development researchers and scientists are reluctant to speak in favor of a ban.

Other equally well-respected and highly credentialed scientists and practitioners are convinced enough by the state of research in this area, and by their clinical experiences, to support a ban. They see it as not only being warranted based on the full spectrum of scientific evidence. They view the ban as a necessary first step in orienting and educating all parents about using non-physical force methods of child rearing.

Alternatives to Corporal Punishment

Those who are advocating for the proposed ban also remind us that there are parents of all cultural and religious groups who never use any type of corporal punishment and whose children grow up to be fine citizens. They propose that parents who are still using spanking and the other varieties of physical punishment consider doing some of the following:

- Analyze the situations where a child is engaging in unwanted behaviors or refusing to do what they are supposed to do to see if the parent can make a change in the situation or environment that will avoid or prevent the unwanted behavior or the refusal to comply.

- Analyze the unwanted behaviors themselves to determine what the opposite or incompatible behaviors are, and focus instead on praising, encouraging, or providing positive I-messages for those incompatible, cooperative behaviors.

- Draw attention away from problematic situations through the use of distraction.

- Use clear and succinct commands and strong body posture to let the child know you are serious about the unwanted behavior stopping.

- Use time out procedures which are discussed and carefully planned in advance.

- Take away privileges and rewards for noncompliance.

- Problem solve and negotiate solutions with the children.

- Organize the family environment so that children earn their privileges and rewards based on their good will and cooperation in complying with mutually agreed upon family rules and values. These ban proponents further urge parents to enroll in parenting classes where these alternatives to corporal punishment can be properly learned and utilized.

Society's Overall Values Regarding Children

This entire debate emanates from the need to justify or not justify the use of physical punishment with children, a debate that has already been decided when the reference is adults, as well as when referring to adults in prisons and jails.

Quite simply, with older human beings, regardless of what they have done, people are not for hitting. With little human beings, the most vulnerable and defenseless of our nation, we are still debating whether they are not for hitting.

What does this say about our character regarding the treatment of children?

It says to all of us, regardless of religious or cultural backgrounds and beliefs, that we have not been appealing to the better angels of our character.

Given the state of the world—and given that the United States has just been ranked by UNICEF as one of the worst places to be a child—isn't it time that we appeal to those better angels?

Let's stop debating, and give our children the same right to be free of physical punishment that we adults have been reserving for ourselves.

"Parents are not stupid, they know the difference between beating and spanking."

Spanking Should Not Be Illegal

Debra Saunders

A proposed bill in California to ban corporal punishment of children sparked a debate over the efficacy and morality of spanking and other forms of corporal punishment. In this viewpoint Debra Saunders argues against the proposed legislation. She maintains that the state should instead focus on true cases of abuse, that a spanking ban would be difficult to enforce, and that parents know the difference between spanking and child abuse. Debra Saunders is a nationally syndicated columnist for The National Ledger, *an online independent news publication.*

As you read, consider the following questions:

1. What arguments does California Assemblywoman Sally Lieber use to defend a spanking ban?
2. According to state law, workers in which professions are required to report suspected child abuse to the proper authorities?

Debra Saunders, "California Spanking Law Proposal Is Absurd," *The National Ledger,* January 20, 2007. Reproduced by permission.

3. According to retired police chief Joseph McNamara, in what instances might spanking be appropriate?

Democratic California Assemblywoman Sally Lieber has announced that she will introduce a bill this week [Jan. 20, 2007] to make it a crime to spank children who are 3 years old or younger, punishable by up to a year in jail or a $1,000 fine. If this zany idea were to become law, California could be the place where the nanny state meets the authoritarian state.

It is more than ironic that a politician who wants to make it illegal for parents to apply their flat hands to their babies' bare bottoms is more than happy to allow the heavy hand of the law to yank parents from their homes and place them behind bars for disciplining their own children in the way that they see fit and does not injure a child.

"I think we ought to have a law against beating children," Lieber told *The San Francisco Chronicle* last week.

That's the problem. California does have laws against beating children. But in this politically correct atmosphere, do-gooders believe it is their right to pass laws that expand definitions beyond reason so that a spanking is a beating—when it isn't.

In effect, this is what Lieber really is saying in proposing such a law: I know how to raise your kids, and I am going to make it illegal for other parents to discipline their children in a way I do not like. If you don't do it my way, you can go to jail.

That's not how Lieber sees it, of course. She told me, "I haven't heard any convincing arguments as to why anyone would want to swat a 6-month-old or 1-year-old." As Lieber sees it, spanking is "not effective," as children under 3 "don't understand it." And: Spanking trains children "in violence and domination, even when it's moderate."

Distinguishing Spanking from Abuse

	Spanking	Physical Abuse
The Act	Spanking: One or two spanks to the buttocks	Beating: To strike repeatedly (also kick, punch, choke)
The Intent	Training: To correct problem behavior	Violence: Physical force intended to injure or abuse
The Attitude	With love and concern	With anger and malice
The Effects	Behavioral correction	Emotional and physical injury

Den A. Trumbull and S. DuBose Ravenel,
"Spare the Rod? New Research Challenges Spanking Critic,"
Family Policy, October 1996, vol. 9, no. 5,
http://faculty.biola.edu/paulp/spare_the_rod.htm.

While Lieber may believe that she is trying to protect children, it's hard to see how a big fine or putting mom or dad in jail for a spanking could be even remotely in a toddler's interest.

Police Are Busy Enough

Let me be clear. I am not defending spanking. Like Lieber, I don't think spanking is effective, and there are better ways to discipline children.

I just happen to believe that California cops have their hands full dealing with adults who beat, torture or otherwise abuse children. Take the case of Oakland's Chazarus Hill Sr., 27, who beat his 3-year-old son Chazarus "Cha Cha" Hill Jr. to death in 2003 after the poor boy wet his bed and made mistakes recognizing flash cards.

Cha Cha had been beaten repeatedly before his father killed him—and I want police to concentrate on finding and going after adults like Hill. California law rightly gives law enforcement the tools to prosecute such parents—and it is on such cases, of bodily injury, that the law should and must focus.

Indeed, state law mandates that teachers, health-care professionals and cops report suspected child abuse to the proper authorities.

Lieber mentioned the Hill case over the phone—which is wrong-headed because Hill was beating his son with deadly weapons, switches and belts, for weeks before he killed him.

A Spanking Ban Would Be Difficult to Enforce

Joseph D. McNamara, a retired police chief of San Jose, Calif., and now a research fellow at Stanford's Hoover Institution, told me that if he were a beat cop, he would be "horrified" at the prospect of enforcing a spanking ban.

Such a law would put police in "everyone's living rooms," where they would have to regulate parenting. Or as Gov. Arnold Schwarzenegger so aptly put it when first told about the proposed law, "How do you enforce that?"

McNamara told me he never spanked his children, but he could conceive of instances in which good parents might choose to do so. Say a parent repeatedly tells a young child not to run into the street, or not to talk to strangers, or to stop hurting a younger sibling—and words alone have not worked.

In such cases, parents—not a Sacramento lawmaker—know what best to do. And while Lieber told me she wants to draw a line that makes physical discipline a "black and white" issue, California parents have been dealing with shades of gray since before Lieber was in diapers. Parents are not stupid, they know the difference between beating and spanking, and they do not need her to draw the line for them.

A Slippery Slope

What's next—McNamara wondered—a law against grabbing your kid by the arm? Pass such laws, he added, and you'll see a state in which "parents are afraid to discipline the child." As if that would be good for California families.

Lieber's response is that wife-beating once was off-limits to law enforcement, but in this enlightened age, the law does come between a man's fist and his wife's face. Again, she fails to distinguish between beating and spanking.

Just as some people choose not to distinguish between physical and verbal abuse.

Lieber explained: "Things have changed. Now we tell parents what to do and what not to do." The state makes adults use car seats for children, and there are laws to keep them away from lead-based paint.

Except spanking doesn't cause physical harm, as car accidents and lead paint can. And if spanking does injure children, it is illegal. This is more about philosophy than safety—and California lawmakers don't have a right to mandate how parents think about raising their own kids. Those who want the government to stay out of the bedroom should not want it in the nursery or at the kitchen table, either.

> "An obsessive concentration on sexual abuse by priests is in danger of blinding us to all their other forms of child abuse."

Religion Is Child Abuse

Richard Dawkins

This first decade of the twenty-first century has been met with scandalous cases of sexual child abuse by Roman Catholic priests. The author of this viewpoint, however, looks at another kind of child abuse from our religious leaders: the emotional abuse rendered by using threats of Hell. Using personal narratives, Richard Dawkins compares the aftermath of physical sexual abuse and the aftermath of the doctrine of Hell. He argues that the consequences of both involve psychological damage, with sexual abuse being the lesser of the two evils. Dawkins, a noted atheist, is a professor at Oxford University and the author of God Delusion, *a best-selling book.*

As you read, consider the following questions:

1. Richard Dawkins begins the viewpoint with a woman's experience of sexual abuse by a priest. At the same age,

Richard Dawkins, "Religion's Real Child Abuse," *RichardDawkins.net*, May 15, 2006. Reproduced by permission.

what mental abuse did she suffer from the same priest, and why was it worse than the sexual abuse?

2. What personal experience has shaped Dawkins' view-point?

3. Psychologist Nicholas Humphrey argues that we should work to free the children of the world from what?

In the wake of the current scandal over child abuse by priests, I have had a letter from an American woman in her mid forties who was brought up Roman Catholic. She has two strong recollections from when she was seven. She was sexu-ally abused by her parish priest in his car. And around the same time a little school friend of hers, who had tragically died, went to hell because she was a Protestant. Or so my cor-respondent was led to believe by the then official doctrine of her church. Her view now is that, of these two examples of Roman Catholic child abuse, the one physical and the other mental, the second was by far the worst. She writes:

> "Being fondled by the priest simply left the impression (from the mind of a 7 year old) as 'yuchy' while the memory of my friend going to hell was one of cold, immeasurable fear. I never lost sleep because of the priest—but I spent many a night being terrified that the people I loved would go to Hell. It gave me nightmares."

I am sure her experience is far from unique. And what if we assume a less altruistic child, worried about her own eter-nity rather than a friend's? Odious as the physical abuse of children by priests undoubtedly is, I suspect that it may do them less lasting damage than the mental abuse of bringing them up Catholic in the first place.

A Personal Account

Happily I was spared the misfortune of a Roman Catholic up-bringing (Anglicanism is a significantly less noxious strain of the virus). Being fondled by the Latin master in the Squash

Court was a disagreeable sensation for a nine-year-old, a mixture of embarrassment and skin-crawling revulsion, but it was certainly not in the same league as being led to believe that I, or someone I knew, might go to everlasting fire. As soon as I could wriggle off his knee, I ran to tell my friends and we had a good laugh, our fellowship enhanced by the shared experience of the same sad pedophile. I do not believe that I, or they, suffered lasting, or even temporary damage from this disagreeable physical abuse of power. Given the Latin Master's eventual suicide, maybe the damage was all on his side.

All Cases of Abuse Are Not the Same

Of course I accept that his misdemeanors, although by today's standards enough to earn imprisonment followed by a life sentence of persecution by vigilantes, were mild compared to those committed by some priests now in the news. I am in no position to make light of the horrific experiences of their altar-boy victims. But reports of child abuse cover a multitude of sins, from mild fondling to violent buggery, and I am sure many of those cases now embarrassing the church fall at the mild end of the spectrum. Doubtless, too, some fall at the violent end, which is terrible but I would make two points about it. First, just because some pedophile assaults are violent and painful, it doesn't mean that all are. A child too young to notice what is happening at the hands of a gentle pedophile will have no difficulty at all in noticing the pain inflicted by a violent one. Phrases like 'predatory monster' are not discriminating enough, and are framed in the light of adult hang-ups. Second (and this is the point with which I began) the *mental* abuse constituted by an unsubstantiated *threat* of violence and terrible pain, if sincerely *believed* by the child, could easily be more damaging than the physical actuality of sexual abuse. An extreme threat of violence and pain is precisely what the doctrine of hell is. And there is no doubt at all that many children sincerely believe it, often continuing right through adulthood and old age until death finally releases them.

buse Leaves More Scars
/sical Abuse

˺ said that the Catholic Church no longer preaches
hell fire in its full horror. That depends on how upmarket is
your area and how progressive your priest. But eternal punishment certainly was the normal doctrine dished out to con-
gregations, including terrified children, back in the time when
many of the priests now facing expulsion or prosecution committed their physical abuses. Most of the victims bringing or
supporting lawsuits are now in their middle years. They therefore, along with many others who were never physically
abused, probably experienced mental terrorism of the hell fire
type. The long retrospect of the law entitles middle-aged victims to lucrative redress, decades after they suffered physically.
Nobody thinks the physical injuries of sexual abuse could possibly last decades, so the damages now being claimed have to
be the mental consequences of the original physical abuse. A
typical claimant, now 54, said that his "life was marred by in-
explicable confusions, anger, depression and lost faith."
(Parenthetically, one can't help marvelling at the idea of a life
being *marred* by lost faith. Perhaps it would get the sympathy
of a jury.) But the point is this. If you can sue for the long-
term mental damage caused by *physical* child abuse, why
should you not sue for the long-term mental damage caused
by *mental* child abuse? Only a minority of priests abuse the
bodies of the children in their care. But how many priests
abuse their minds? Why aren't Catholics and ex-Catholics lin-
ing up to sue the church into the ground, for a lifetime of
psychological damage?

A Distraction

I am not advocating this course of action. Much as I would
like to see the Roman Catholic Church ruined, I hate oppor-
tunistically retrospective litigation even more. Lawyers who
grow fat by digging dirt on long-forgotten wrongs, and hound-

Major Religions of the World Ranked by Number of Adherents

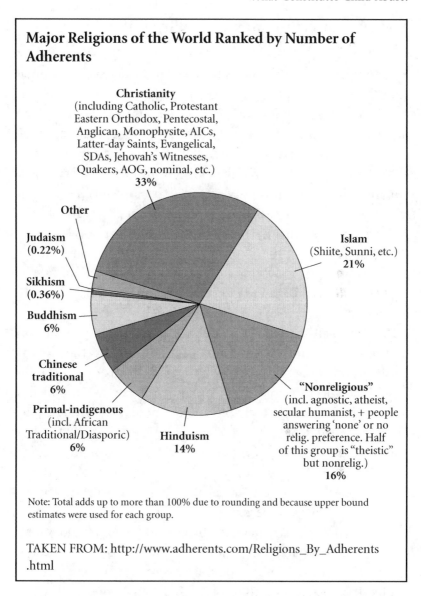

Christianity
(including Catholic, Protestant
Eastern Orthodox, Pentecostal,
Anglican, Monophysite, AICs,
Latter-day Saints, Evangelical,
SDAs, Jehovah's Witnesses,
Quakers, AOG, nominal, etc.)
33%

Other

Judaism
(0.22%)

Islam
(Shiite, Sunni, etc.)
21%

Sikhism
(0.36%)

Buddhism
6%

**Chinese
traditional
6%**

"Nonreligious"
(incl. agnostic, atheist,
secular humanist, + people
answering 'none' or no
relig. preference. Half
of this group is "theistic"
but nonrelig.)
16%

Primal-indigenous
(incl. African
Traditional/Diasporic)
6%

**Hinduism
14%**

Note: Total adds up to more than 100% due to rounding and because upper bound
estimates were used for each group.

TAKEN FROM: http://www.adherents.com/Religions_By_Adherents
.html

ing their aged perpetrators, are no friends of mine. All I am
doing is calling attention to an anomaly. By all means, let's
kick a nasty institution when it is down, but there are better
ways than litigation. And an obsessive concentration on *sexual*
abuse by priests is in danger of blinding us to all their other
forms of child abuse.

The Mental Abuse Makes the Physical Abuse Possible

The threat of eternal hell is an extreme example of mental abuse, just as violent sodomy is an extreme example of physical abuse. Most physical abuse is milder, and so is most of the mental abuse inherent in a typical religious education. The priest who urged a 14-year-old altar boy to give him oral sex, "blessing it as a way to receive Holy Communion" wasn't only abusing the trust normally enjoyed by any teacher, youth leader or scoutmaster. He was cashing in on the years of religious brainwashing that the child had endured as a cradle Catholic. Holy Communion: nice one! But again, only an extreme example of what churches—and also mosques and synagogues—do to child minds in their care, in the normal course of events.

'What shall we tell the children?' is a superb polemic on how religions abuse the minds of children, by the distinguished psychologist Nicholas Humphrey. It was originally delivered as a lecture in aid of Amnesty International, and has now been reissued as a chapter of his book, *The Mind Made Flesh*, published by Oxford University Press [in 2002]. It is also available on the worldwide web, and I strongly recommend it. Humphrey argues that, in the same way as Amnesty works tirelessly to free political prisoners the world over, we should work to free the children of the world from the religions which, with parental approval, damage minds too young to understand what is happening to them. He is right, and the same lesson should inform our discussions of the current pedophile brouhaha. Priestly groping of child bodies is disgusting. But it may be less harmful in the long run than priestly subversion of child minds.

"Our own legal tradition ... has long upheld 'the fundamental interest of parents, as contrasted with that of the State, to guide the religious future and education of their children.'"

Religion Is Not Child Abuse

ParentalRights.org

The United Nations Convention on the Rights of the Child (U.N. CRC) has come under fire by parental rights organizations who believe that it goes too far and jeopardizes the rights of parents, especially regarding religious instruction. This viewpoint cites experts who oppose the CRC and argue against the United States' ratification of it. ParentalRights.org is an organization dedicated to supporting a constitutional amendment that protects the parental-child relationship from unreasonable intrusion.

As you read, consider the following questions:

1. According to Cynthia Price Cohen, what was deleted from an earlier draft of Article 14 of the United Nation's Convention on the Rights of the Child?

2. What, according to Nicholas Humphry, is the role of the parent?

3. According to Innaiah Narisetti, what organization should not belong in the United Nations?

The United Nations Convention on the Rights of the Child [U.N. CRC], in Article 14, says that the government shall "respect the right of the child to freedom of thought, conscience and religion," and shall also "respect the rights and duties of the parents and, when applicable, legal guardians, to provide direction to the child in the exercise of his or her right in a manner consistent with the evolving capacities of the child."

Proponents of the CRC, such as law professor Jonathan Todres, have commented that Article 14 "provides for the role of parents in teaching religion to their children, while ensuring that the government does not impose restrictions on any child's right to freedom of religion." Nevertheless, a deeper understanding of this provision reveals that the purportedly "pro-parent" language is really another avenue for government power, not a shield to protect parental rights.

How Much "Direction" Is Too Much Direction?

On its face, this article may seem to support the role of parents, but such a position is merely wishful thinking. The Convention merely recognizes the parents' primary role to "provide direction" to the child, and there is considerable disagreement on what this "direction" should entail. For example, according to Faulkner University law professor John Garman, Article 14 is one of the few clauses in the CRC that "actually brings the parents into play to 'provide direction to the child.'"

But another CRC proponent, law professor Cynthia Price Cohen, disagrees. According to Cohen, one of the earliest drafts of Article 14 included "two paragraphs that protected the right of parents to guide the exercise of this right and to

United Nations Convention on the Rights of the Child: Article 14

Article 14

1. States Parties shall respect the right of the child to freedom of thought, conscience and religion.

2. States Parties shall respect the rights and duties of the parents and, when applicable, legal guardians, to provide direction to the child in the exercise of his or her right in a manner consistent with the evolving capacities of the child.

3. Freedom to manifest one's religion or beliefs may be subject only to such limitations as are prescribed by law and are necessary to protect public safety, order, health or morals, or the fundamental rights and freedoms of others.

Office of the United Nations High Commissioner for Human Rights, http://www2.ohchr.org/english/law/crc.htm.

'respect the liberty of the child and his parents' with regard to the child's religious education." When the final text was adopted, however, all language protecting the rights of parents to "ensure the religious and moral education of the child" was omitted. This omission makes no sense if the purpose of Article 14 was to protect the rights of *parents* to instruct their children.

Religious "Indoctrination" as Abuse?

The danger to parents is compounded by a growing movement among American and international academics to prevent parents from "indoctrinating" their children with religious beliefs. For example, British scientist and bestselling author Richard Dawkins recently described religious "indoctrination" of young children as a form of child abuse. "Odious as the physical abuse of children by priests undoubtedly is," Dawkins writes, "I suspect that it may do them less lasting damage than the mental abuse of bringing them up Catholic in the first place."

Dawkins is not alone in his analysis. In 1998, bestselling author and professor of psychology Nicholas Humphrey, teaching at New York University at the time, argued for "censorship" of parents, who have "no right to limit the horizons of their children's knowledge, to bring them up in an atmosphere of dogma and superstition, or to insist they follow the straight and narrow paths of their own faith."

Both authors advocate an outside solution to "protect" children from indoctrination: intervention by the government. In *The God Delusion*, Dawkins quotes from Humphrey, who writes that "children have a right not to have their minds addled by nonsense, and *we as a society have a duty to protect them from it*." Humphrey bluntly adds that "parents' rights have no status in ethics and should have none in law"— parenting is a "privilege" that operates within parameters set by *society* to protect the child's "fundamental rights to self-determination." If parents step beyond these boundaries by indoctrinating their children, "the contract lapses—and *it is then the duty of those who granted the privilege to intervene*." (emphasis added)

Some have called for international talks on whether children should be involved in religion. Innaiah Narisetti of the Center for Inquiry (a U.N. NGO [Non-Governmental Organization]) said, "The time has come to debate the participation of children in religious institutions." Continues Narisetti, "While some might see it as a matter better left to parents, the negative influence of religion and its subsequent contribution to child abuse from religious beliefs and practices requires us to ask whether organized religion is an institution that needs limits set on how early it should have access to children." Narisetti also said that "The UN must then take a clear stand on the issue of the forced involvement of children in religious practices; it must speak up for the rights of children and not the automatic right of parents and societies to pass on religious beliefs, and it must reexamine whether an organization like the Vatican should belong to the UN."

The "Fundamental Interest of Parents"

This aggressive censorship of parents captures the true spirit of Article 14. According to law professor Bruce Hafen, the language of Article 14 views "parents as trustees of the state who have only such authority and discretion as the state may grant in order to protect the child's independent rights," and is consistent with what the state deems as the child's "evolving capacities." Such a calloused view of parents stands in stark contrast to our own legal tradition, which has long upheld "the fundamental interest of parents, as contrasted with that of the State, to guide the religious future and education of their children."

America's legal heritage has consistently held that *parents* have a fundamental right to teach their children about religion, shielded from well-intentioned but intrusive interference from the state. The danger of Article 14 is that it disrupts this crucial balance, tipping the scales in favor of the government and those who claim to "know better" in our society. If we wish to secure these freedoms, we must act now to place parental rights into the text of our Constitution.

> "There is increasing concern about the negative impact on children when parents ... abuse alcohol or drugs or engage in other illegal drug-related activity, such as the manufacture of methamphetamines on home-based laboratories."

Parental Drug Use Is Considered a Criminal Act in Some States

Child Welfare Information Gateway

Recognizing the danger posed to children by parents who abuse drugs, most states have laws addressing the issues of prenatal and postnatal drug exposure. This viewpoint provides an overview of some of the policies and procedures that states have enacted to respond to substance-exposed newborns, and it illustrates how some states have broadened their legal definition of child abuse and neglect to include exposing children to illegal drug activity. The Child Welfare Information Gateway is a service of the Children's Bureau, Administration for Children and Families, U.S. Department of Health and Human Services.

"Parental Drug Use as Child Abuse," *Child Welfare Information Gateway*, August 23, 2007.

As you read, consider the following questions:

1. What are the two primary areas of concern regarding parental use of illegal substances?
2. What does the Child Abuse Prevention and Treatment Act require of states?
3. List three examples of what some states consider drug-related child abuse or neglect.

Abuse of drugs or alcohol by parents and other caretakers can have a negative impact on the health, safety, and well-being of children. Approximately 45 States, the District of Columbia, and Guam currently have laws within their child protection statutes that address the issue of substance abuse by parents. Two main areas of concern are (1) the harm caused by prenatal drug exposure and (2) the harm caused to children of any age by exposure to illegal drug activity in the home.

Prenatal Drug Exposure

The Child Abuse Prevention and Treatment Act (CAPTA) requires States to have policies and procedures in place to notify CPS [Child Protective Services] of substance-exposed newborns (SENs) and to establish a plan of safe care for newborns identified as being affected by illegal substance abuse or withdrawal symptoms resulting from prenatal drug exposure. Several States currently address this requirement in their statutes. Approximately 15 States and the District of Columbia have specific reporting procedures for infants who show evidence at birth of having been exposed to drugs, alcohol, or other controlled substances, while 13 States and the District of Columbia include this type of exposure in their definitions of child abuse or neglect.

Some States specify in statute the response the CPS agency must make to reports of substance-exposed newborns. Hawaii and Maine require the State agency to develop a plan of safe care for the infant. California, Maryland, Missouri, Nevada, and the District of Columbia require the agency to complete an assessment of the needs of the infant and the infant's family and make a referral to appropriate services. Illinois and Minnesota require mandated reporters to report when they suspect that pregnant women are substance abusers, so that the women can be referred for treatment.

Children Exposed to Illegal Drug Activity

There is increasing concern about the negative impact on children when parents or other members of the household abuse alcohol or drugs or engage in other illegal drug-related activity, such as the manufacture of methamphetamines in home-based laboratories. Many States have responded to this problem by expanding the civil definition of child abuse or neglect. Specific circumstances that are considered child abuse or neglect in some States include:

- The manufacture of a controlled substance in the presence of a child or on the premises occupied by a child

- Allowing a child to be present where the chemicals or equipment for the manufacture of controlled substances are used or stored

- Selling, distributing, or giving drugs or alcohol to a child

- The use of a controlled substance by a caregiver that impairs the caregiver's ability to adequately care for the child

- The exposure of the child to drug paraphernalia

- The exposure to the criminal sale or distribution of drugs

- The exposure to drug-related activity.

Methamphetamine: Children at Risk

If a pregnant woman uses meth, the baby may experience:

- Premature birth
- Low birth weight
- Cerebral injuries
- Birth defects (up to 6 times more likely) including effects on the central nervous system, heart and kidneys
- Cerebral palsy and paralysis
- Dopamine depletion
- Abnormal sleep patterns
- Poor feeding
- Limpness
- Apparent depression
- Shaking and tremors
- Irritability
- Fits of rage
- Sensitivity to stimuli including human touch and regular light
- Coordination problems

In cases where an intervention is done and the child receives appropriate services, the child may not experience any significant long-term effects.

Kansas Methamphetamine Prevention Project,
http://www.ksmethpreventionproject.org/
Children%20at%20Risk.pdf.

Criminal Statutes

Approximately 23 States address the issue of exposing children to illegal drug activity in their criminal statutes. For example, in Georgia, Illinois, Nebraska, New Hampshire, Pennsylvania, Virginia, West Virginia, and Wyoming, the manufacture or possession of methamphetamine in the presence of a child is a felony, while in Idaho, Louisiana, and Ohio, the manufacture or possession of any controlled substance in the presence of a child is considered a felony. California, Mississippi, Montana, North Carolina, and Washington State have enacted enhanced penalties for any conviction for the manufacture of methamphetamine when a child was present on the premises where the crime occurred.

Exposing children to the manufacture, possession, or distribution of illegal drugs is considered child endangerment in Alaska, Iowa, Kansas, Minnesota, and Missouri. The exposure of a child to drugs or drug paraphernalia is a crime in North Dakota and Utah. In North Carolina and Wyoming, selling or giving an illegal drug to a child by any person is a felony.

> *"In this century we ... know enough about addiction to understand that addiction comes bundled with a host of other problems that require treatment, not arrest."*

Parental Drug Use Should Not Be Considered a Criminal Act

Sarah Blustain

Hundreds of women have been arrested and charged with murder after delivering babies who test positively for illegal drugs and who die before or shortly after birth. In this viewpoint, Sarah Blustain argues that these arrests are inappropriate because there is to date no evidence linking prenatal drug use to stillbirth and because there is a lack of legislation equating prenatal drug use with murder. Further, Blustain argues that arrests and legislation do not help women, but deter women from getting the help they need. Sarah Blustain is a senior editor at The New Republic.

As you read, consider the following questions:

1. What was Theresa Hernandez originally charged with after the stillbirth of her baby who tested positively for methamphetamines?

2. Hundreds of women have been charged with murder after delivering stillborn babies or babies who have died shortly after birth. According to the author, Sarah Blustain, what are these prosecutions the result of?

3. According to researchers, what seems to be the effect of taking a punitive approach to drug-addicted pregnant women?

There's no doubt that 30-year-old Theresa Hernandez has had her troubles. An intermittent user of methamphetamines, she had her 32-week pregnancy end in April 2004 with the birth of a stillborn boy. But "troubles" doesn't begin to describe what came next:

Doctors told police her stillborn baby had tested positive for meth, and that September Hernandez was charged with first- and second-degree murder, both based on child abuse. It was the first time in Oklahoma history that a woman had ever been prosecuted for murder after suffering a stillbirth—despite the absence of evidence tying meth use to prematurity or stillbirth.

The situation got even worse. Hernandez's public defender recommended that she accept a 25-year plea bargain—despite the fact that Oklahoma has no laws under which she might have been convicted of murder. Hernandez refused, and spent three years in jail awaiting a resolution to her case. This September Hernandez accepted a plea of second-degree murder; her sentencing, which the judge has said will be for no more than 15 years, is scheduled for Dec. 21 [2007]. Advocates are agitating for leniency.

No Link Between Meth and Stillbirth

In the words of Lynn Paltrow, a women's rights advocate involved in the case, Hernandez was "an innocent woman pleading guilty to a nonexistent crime." Innocent, you wonder? Guilty, clearly, of taking illegal drugs. And of killing her child? Though long-term, government-funded studies of meth have not yet been completed, there is to date no research associating meth use with stillbirth. Indeed, long-term studies of those infamous crack babies has found that their *in utero* drug exposure led to some behavioral problems, but not to the grotesque abnormalities predicted in the 1980s. And of killing her child *in the first degree*? In this century we also know enough about addiction to understand that addiction comes bundled with a host of other problems that require treatment, not arrest.

Many More Cases

Still, despite these advances in understanding, Hernandez's case is not unique. According to a survey that will be released in 2008 by Paltrow's organization, the National Advocates for Pregnant Women, over the last 30 years hundreds of pregnant women have been arrested for abuse, neglect, or murder of their fetuses. In South Carolina, scores of pregnant women caught abusing substances have been prosecuted for child abuse and neglect, and the first woman convicted of murdering her unborn by virtue of her drug use. Regina McKnight, is serving a 12-year sentence for suffering a premature stillbirth, despite evidence that the baby died from other causes. This October another South Carolina woman, Lorraine Patrick, was charged with homicide after she went into labor at 23 weeks and gave birth to a girl who died four days later; she and the baby tested positive for cocaine.

Punishing Mothers Does Not Help Children

Women's and children's advocates agree that women should engage in behaviors that promote the birth of healthy children. Nevertheless, they recognize that a woman's substance abuse involves complex factors that must be addressed in a constructive manner. Punitive approaches fail to resolve addiction problems and ultimately undermine the health and well-being of women and their children. For this reason, public health groups and medical organizations uniformly oppose measures that treat pregnant women with substance abuse problems as criminals. Moreover, courts have repeatedly rejected attempts to prosecute women under existing criminal laws for their prenatal actions, impose restrictions on women's activities because they are fertile or pregnant, or coerce women to undergo medical procedures to benefit their fetuses. Some of these decisions have explicitly recognized that the fetal rights theory poses a significant threat to women's reproductive rights and the best interests of children.

Lynn M. Paltrow, "Punishing Women
for their Behavior During Pregnancy: An Approach
That Undermines the Health of Women and Children,"
Cora Lee Wetherington and Adele B. Roman (editors),
Drug Addiction Research and the Health of Women,
Department of Health and Human Services, 1998, pp. 467–501.

Fetal-Rights Laws

These prosecutions are clearly the offspring of the crack-babies craze of the 1980s, paired, equally clearly, with the application of fetal-rights laws around the country. If a fetus is considered a "child in utero" (language from the 2004 Unborn

Victims of Violence Act) and an independent victim of murder, how much imagination would it take for an aggressive district attorney to suggest that a pregnant woman using drugs is assaulting, or killing, her own child? No legislature has enacted laws to this effect. (South Carolina's orgy of prosecutions is the result of judicial decisions.) And more than 20 appellate courts have struck these arrests down. And yet they continue, and women serve time for nonexistent crimes.

Punishment Does Not Help

Of course, humane people agree as to our obligation to protect the unborn. But these arrests don't do that: Researchers have documented that taking a punitive approach to drug use among pregnant women, rather than inspiring them to get clean, actually scares them away from prenatal treatment.

And what of the mother? Do the responsibilities she has in carrying a child absolve us of the responsibility to grant her certain protections and rights? Like the right to be jailed only for an actual crime or the right to be convicted on actual evidence? And what about the expectation, though not a right, of social supports, for poverty or drug addiction? These supports are part of our social compact, and we owe them equally, or doubly, to pregnant women. The guilty pleas most of the arrested women have entered in these cases create no legal precedent, but, says Paltrow, the more general precedent that's being set is "that a fetus is a person to be provided with a perfect environment by the pregnant woman—even though [the pregnant woman] is not entitled to one."

It is possible to help both mother and fetus. But not if a troubled woman is considered a demon, or a walking womb.

> "No specific law protects siblings from other siblings and . . . protection can only be obtained when a parent files charges against the abuser on behalf of the victim."

Sibling Bullying Is Child Abuse

Shelley Eriksen and Vickie Jensen

Too often regarded as "normal," sibling violence is more common than any other form of family violence. This viewpoint discusses the effects of sibling violence; explains the differences between sibling rivalry and sibling violence; and presents family characteristics, family resources, and family disorganization as factors that set the stage for sibling violence. The authors, Shelley Eriksen and Vickie Jensen are sociology professors at California State University.

As you read, consider the following questions:

1. Who do perpetrators of sibling violence tend to act violent toward later in life?

Shelley Eriksen and Vickie Jensen, "All in the Family? Family Environmental Factors in Sibling Violence," *Journal of Family Violence*, 2006, vol. 21, pp. 497–507. Copyright © 2006 Springer Science + Business Media, Inc. Reproduced by permission of the publisher and authors.

2. What is the difference between sibling rivalry and sibling assault?

3. What are the three different results of studies examining the effect of family size on the frequency of family violence?

Sibling violence is the least studied form of family violence, but is likely the most prevalent. [Murray] Straus, [Richard J.] Gelles, and [Suzanne K.] Steinmetz were the first to call attention to sibling violence as a widespread and problematic phenomenon. Based on findings from their survey "Physical Violence in American Families, 1976," they suggested that the sibling relationship, rather than the husband/wife or parent/child dyad [a pair of individuals], was the more likely milieu [setting] in which a family member might be victimized. When applied to the nation's estimated 36.3 million children ages 3–17 in their survey year, Straus and Gelles extrapolated that over 29 million American children engage in one or more acts of physical violence toward a sibling.

Lasting Effects

Although the prevalence of sibling abuse in childhood has yet to be systematically explored using more recent, representative data, a limited amount of clinical research suggests that sibling violence can be associated with severe emotional and behavioral problems in children. [G.R.] Patterson, [T.J.] Dishion, and [L.] Bank find that boys' coercive behavior toward a sibling is linked to antisocial behavior among peers and rejection by peers. Similarly, [R.] Duncan finds a significant relationship between peer bullying and sibling bullying, with children who experience both suffering negative emotional consequences.

Some researchers suggest that sibling violence is associated with later negative psychosocial outcomes in adulthood. For example, studies find that childhood sibling violence is associated with later violent behavior in relationships with intimates, peers, and as parents. Among clinicians who study adults, sibling violence is thought to have long-lasting and damaging effects on relational ties among adult brothers and sisters. Several studies also find that sibling violence underlies other emotional and behavioral problems among young adults. For example, [Sandra A.] Graham-Bermann, [S.] Cutler, [B.] Litzenberger, and [W.E.] Schwartz found that women college students who were the earlier target of a sibling's mild or severe violence exhibited higher rates of anxiety in young adulthood than those who did not. [V.] Jensen reports that young adults, especially males, in her college sample who were perpetrators of sibling abuse, before and after the age of 12, exhibited more frequent drug usage and heavier alcohol consumption. . . .

The Lack of Research

Several researchers have noted that sibling violence is understudied and underreported. Sibling violence remains understudied for several reasons. Gelles and [C.P.] Cornell note that siblings' hitting each other is so common that few people regard it as deviant behavior. Indeed, they observe that many American parents believe that sibling aggression facilitates their children's learning how to successfully manage aggressive behavior in future non-family relationships. [W.] DesKeseredy and [D.] Ellis, drawing from Canadian as well as U.S. research, echo this observation, stating that most find such conflict an inevitable part of sibling relations.

Sibling Rivalry

Social norms further encourage expressions of aggressive behavior between siblings. Most of siblings' aggressive behavior, of course, is thought to be attributable to normal sibling rivalry, something children presumably outgrow and adults inevitably forget. However, research on sibling rivalry is woefully underdeveloped, both as a childhood phenomenon and as a continuing dimension of adult sibling relationships. Its inconsistent operationalization across studies also renders spurious any claims to its universality. Nevertheless, this notion of siblings as "rivals"—a concept popularized by psychoanalytic theory—continues to drive most discussions of sibling relationships in lay and scholarly circles, minimizing as it does acts of aggression that would otherwise be considered assaults in any other family or personal relationship.

Sibling Assault

Drawing from clinical practice, [John V.] Caffaro and [Allison] Conn-Caffaro note that sibling rivalry is insufficient to fully explain sibling assault. Rivalry, they argue, includes conflict between siblings that involves possession of something the other also wants, a strengthening of the relationship, and balanced comparisons between siblings. Conversely, assault involves repeated patterns of physical aggression with the intent to harm as well as to humiliate and to defeat. Additionally, they describe sibling assault as part of an escalating pattern of sibling aggression and retaliation unchecked by parental intervention, as well as the solidifying of victim and offender roles between siblings. Such comparisons are not found in research other than that drawn from clinical practice, which leaves unexamined the systematic delineation of differences between sibling rivalry and sibling violence.

Sibling Abuse Defined

Researchers have faced many definitional conundrums with the conceptualization of sibling violence. Some, like [H.] Wallace, define sibling abuse as any form of physical, mental or sexual abuse inflicted on one child by another, inclusive of siblings and step-siblings. Noting similar conceptual inconsistencies in the literature on sibling violence, DesKeseredy and Ellis chose to define sibling violence as "intentional physical

violence inflicted by one child in a family unit on another."
[L.] Stock suggests that legal definitions contribute to this
definition problem, because no specific law protects siblings
from other siblings and that such protection can only be obtained when a parent files charges against the abuser on behalf
of the victim. In addition, many studies focus on children,
leaving mid-to-late adolescence and early adulthood less examined as potential periods of sibling violence. There is also a
general tendency in the literature to conflate or use inter-
changeably such terms as abuse, conflict, aggression and violence. . . .

Socio-Demographic and Family Characteristics

Research suggests that age, gender, and family composition are
consequential to the occurrence of sibling violence. Age is the
more consistent predictor of sibling violence, but its actual
configuration of influence remains unclear. Examining
younger children, [D.J.] Pepler, [R.] Abramovitch, and [C.]
Corter found that older siblings (age 4–7) were more likely to
initiate aggression, while younger (age 3) siblings tended to either retaliate or submit. Other research suggests that sibling
aggression declines with age, that siblings tend to fight more
with younger siblings than with older and more frequently
with those closer in age. Yet, others find no effect of age difference on the occurrence of sibling violence.

Gender

Studies also suggest that the gender of the perpetrator and the
gender mix of sibling sets are central variables. Among their
college-aged subjects, [Sandra A.] Graham-Bermann *et al.*,
found that their male subjects reported higher levels of violence perpetration, and the sibling dyad at greatest risk involved an older brother perpetrator and a younger sister victim. [Megan P.] Goodwin and [Bruce] Roscoe similarly found

Some of the Risk Factors for Sibling Abuse

Much more research needs to be done to find out how and why sibling abuse happens. Some risk factors are:

- Parents are not around much at home

- Parents are not very involved in their children's lives, or are emotionally unavailable to them

- Parents accept sibling rivalry as part of family life, rather than working to minimize it

- Parents do not stop children when they are violent (they may assume it was accidental, part of a two-way fight, or normal horseplay)

- Parents increase competition among children by:

  playing favorites

  comparing children

  labeling or type-casting children (even casting kids in positive roles is harmful)

- Parents have not taught children about sexuality and about personal safety

- Parents and children are in denial that there is a problem

- Children have inappropriate family roles, for example, they are burdened with too much care-taking responsibility for a younger sibling

University of Michigan Health Systems,
"Your Child: Sibling Abuse."
www.med.umich.edu/llibr/yourchild/sibabuse.htm.

among their junior and senior high school students that young men as perpetrators threatened to harm their siblings more often and engaged in a wider range of violent acts (e.g. hitting siblings with objects, holding siblings against their will, beating them up, choking and bodily throwing them), although brothers were as likely recipients of these actions as were sisters. [In a 1999 study,] Duncan also found boys reporting significantly more victimization at the hands of sibling bullies than girls. However, other researchers report no significant difference in the perpetration or victimization of physical violence among male and female siblings.

Family Size

Few studies have highlighted directly the effect of family size on the frequency of sibling violence. [M.S.] Hardy found no significant relationship between number of siblings and sibling violence. Other research on child maltreatment in general reports greater violence by parents toward children among families of larger than average family size. Gelles and Straus find the opposite pattern, however. In their national sample, parents with two children had a higher rate of violence toward their offspring than those with larger families.

Family Structure

Related research also suggests that other family structure variables are implicated in the occurrence of sibling violence. Previous investigators report an association between single-parent families and various forms of family violence like child abuse. Similarly, others have found that many of the perpetrators of physical abuse in families were not biologically related to the child, suggesting families are more at risk of violence in divorced, separated or blended families. Direct examination of sibling violence by [M.] Hardy found no significant differences between family composition and sibling violence. However, too few studies have examined the relationship between reconstituted families and sibling violence to establish any pattern.

Thus, while age, gender, and family composition are clearly components of family violence, the ways in which they may augment or diminish sibling violence remains unclear.

Family Resources and Family Stability

Hardy suggested that the effects of family resources and family stability on sibling violence are gleaned from studies on family violence, rather than sibling violence *per se*. Studies of family violence suggest socioeconomic status, part-time employment or unemployment, parents' marriage or divorce, and support networks of kin and community potentially influence violent behavior among siblings.

In general, families who face economic challenges have been shown to have higher rates of family violence. For example, despite the necessary adage that family violence occurs in every social and cultural group, research on family violence in the 1970's and 1980's found that both wife abuse and child abuse were more prevalent among families of lower socioeconomic standing. Along similar lines, others have found that parents who are unemployed, who are employed part time, especially husbands, and who report financial problems run a greater risk of child abuse. Husbands who report low job satisfaction are also linked with higher rates of wife abuse. The National Research Council reported that poverty is strongly associated with child abuse, though the Council report cautions that poverty works within a constellation of factors to increase the likelihood of child abuse. Although some note the possible effect of financial instability on sibling violence, only Hardy has actually found that financial and business stresses, and any work transitions in the family, increase the likelihood of sibling violence.

Social Isolation

The absence of stable employment may add to family stress and a family's social isolation, factors routinely linked with violent families. Consonant with a family stress model, previous research suggests that abusive families are more socially isolated than non-abusive families, particularly those families who have lived in the same neighborhood for less than three years or have fewer ties to organizations outside the home. Indeed, Hardy found families with high amounts of sibling violence were more isolated, with a rigid boundary created between family and outsiders as a result. Lack of affiliation with, or participation in, religious organizations might be especially important in creating an environment for sibling violence. Research finds that husbands' religious affiliation and attendance acts as a potential deterrent to wife abuse.

Family Disorganization

Studies also suggest that sibling violence takes place within a broader context of family violence and disorganization which normalizes aggression among children. Two theoretical models—social learning and family systems theory—suggest, respectively, that children learn how to behave from the actions they see their parents take and that any particular relationship dyad in a family reflects the general tempo and tone of the family constellation as a whole. Taken together, these models direct our attention to the manner in which sibling aggression might mirror, or even be generated by, other forms of violence occurring around children in a family.

Witnesses of Violence

Within this frame, several forms of family violence appear particularly consequential. Researchers studying the intergenerational transmission of violence among men who batter have noted that witnessing parental violence in childhood may be a more important factor in subsequent male-perpetrated attacks than being the direct target of it. This would make sense of research that finds a significant relationship between parental use of severe violence to resolve parental conflict and children's use of severe violence to resolve conflict with each other. However, others argue for a more direct effect, citing evidence of children involved in homicidal attacks on younger siblings who were often themselves victims of parental abuse or neglect. Parallel research reports greater physical and sexual abuse of children from homes in which parent-child conflict was significant. Extant literature in the field of sibling violence that examines the relationship between parental physical abuse of children and sibling violence reaffirms the importance of looking at this particular factor.

Family Power Structure

While both witnessed and actual experience of parental violence are concrete indices of family disorganization, more loosely related factors may also shape levels of sibling violence. For example, research has found that abusive families tend to have higher levels of marital discord and drinking problems, as do abusive husbands. Indeed, Hardy found that marital strain had a significant impact on sibling violence. Less examined is the relative balance of power between husbands and wives, as well as parents' orientation toward corporal punishment, as each may shape a particular relational ethos among children that legitimizes aggression based on presumed authority. In this light, studies suggest that abusive parents are particularly prone to believe in spanking, and that physical punishment is correlated with increased risk of later adult substance abuse and criminal activity. Finally, . . . the domination-submission relationship assumed by more traditional gender role ideology is strongly associated with family violence. . . .

Taken together, disparate research efforts suggest that individual and family characteristics, family resources and stability, and family disorganization are among the more salient environmental factors that underlie violence among siblings.

> "If child poverty was seen as abuse then the number of children [in the United Kingdom] who would be classed as being abused would increase from less than 1 per cent to around 26 per cent."

Poverty Is Child Abuse

Nicola Jose

Child poverty and child abuse, particularly child neglect, are closely related. Whether poverty is self-induced or caused by society is unclear, but in either case it is not the fault of the child. This viewpoint examines the connection between child poverty and child abuse by defining "abuse" and "poverty," explaining the two main theories of the causes of poverty and discussing how classifying child poverty as child abuse would make eradicating child poverty a larger priority for health care and social care professionals. The author, Nicola Jose, is a lecturer in child health and children's nursing at Thames Valley University.

As you read, consider the following questions:

1. What are the two main theories of the causes of poverty?

Nicola Jose, "Child Poverty: Is It Child Abuse?" *Paediatric Nursing*, vol. 17, October 2005, pp. 20–23. Copyright © 2005 Royal College of Nursing Publishing Company. Reproduced by permission.

2. What is the definition of "dependency culture," according to American sociologist Charles Murray?

3. According to the author, Nicola Jose, what would be an advantage of classifying child poverty as child abuse?

The UK [United Kingdom] has one of the highest child poverty rates in the industrialised world: 15.4 per cent of the child population, or an estimated 3.8 million children, live in relative poverty. Campaigning for a reduction in child poverty is high on the agenda of many children's charities and organisations, as the 'Make poverty history' campaign earlier this year [2005] demonstrated. The UK government has made reducing child poverty a priority, pledging to halve these numbers by 2010 and eradicate child poverty by 2020. Child poverty should be of concern to everyone and is of particular importance for healthcare professionals as the impact on children's health of living in poverty can be significant.

Section 17 of the Children Act 1989 states that we all have a duty to safeguard children and protect them from harm. Nurses caring for children and young people have an important role in child protection which was emphasised in the Laming report [report issued in January 2003 by Lord Herbert Laming on the murder of Victoria Climbié, an eight-year-old girl, in London in 2000]. Can child poverty be a cause of harm and therefore should it be classed as a form of abuse? If this is the case then it would be a duty of nurses and other healthcare, professionals to recognise the impact that poverty has on a child and his or her family and act accordingly. This article explores definitions of abuse and poverty and considers whether child poverty could be classed as a form of child abuse.

Child Abuse

In its simplest definition, child abuse can be thought of as ways of treating a child that are harmful or morally wrong. The Department of Health (DH) suggests that 'somebody may abuse or neglect a child by inflicting harm or failing to act to prevent harm'. Child abuse can be classified under four main headings: physical abuse, sexual abuse, emotional abuse and neglect.

Any form of abuse can be difficult to recognise: emotional abuse or neglect in particular can be difficult to categorise and prove as there is often a lack of visible evidence. Cultural differences and values may affect judgements about what is and is not acceptable behaviour. Attitudes to risk taking behaviour, such as children playing in the street, may differ as much according to social class as to availability of, or access to, gardens and local parks. Child abuse occurs in all social classes and across all ethnic groups. However, there are risk factors such as poor housing, poverty and unemployment that can be used as predictors of abuse.

Poverty

Defining poverty can be difficult and definitions take many forms.... In 1886 Charles Booth [a pioneer in poverty studies], identified the very poor as those whose means were insufficient according to the 'normal standards' of life in this country, and this definition is still used today. Most definitions are not specific to children and it is important to realise that child poverty does not exist in isolation: if a child lives in poverty then the family as a whole will be classified as living in poverty. Household income is often used as an indicator of poverty and unemployment has a significant impact on child poverty. The UK has one of the highest proportions of children living in workless and poor households in the EU [European Union] countries. This is perhaps why our child poverty rate is among the highest in the industrialised world.

Indicators of Poverty

Measuring Child Poverty, published in December 2003, introduced new UK definitions of child poverty.

Three indicators are now used to identify and measure child poverty:

- *absolute low income* defined as a child living with two adults whose income is £210 [£210 is approximately equivalent to $416] a week (adjusted annually for inflation). This figure is adjusted to family size and is designed to show if families' incomes are increasing and indicate whether progress is being made

- *relative low income* defined as children living in households whose income is below 60 per cent median equalised household income. This measurement is commonly used within the European Union and allows for comparisons between countries to be made. This measurement is adjusted to reflect changes in income and economic growth

- *material deprivation* incorporates relative low income and relates to a gauge of living standards. A list of essential items that involve social interaction and acceptance has been drawn up to measure this indicator, such as hobbies, leisure pursuits, holidays and seeing friends.

Poverty Is Self Induced

There are a number of standpoints taken as to who or what causes poverty. The main argument focuses on whether individuals cause their own poverty or whether society causes poverty. Oscar Lewis proposed one of the most influential theories of poverty, which is that individuals are responsible for their poverty. He suggested that there is a culture of poverty that exists among the poor and that children are socialised into this cultural way of life. It is transmitted across generations leading to children developing no ambitions, desires or aspirations for their future. The American sociologist

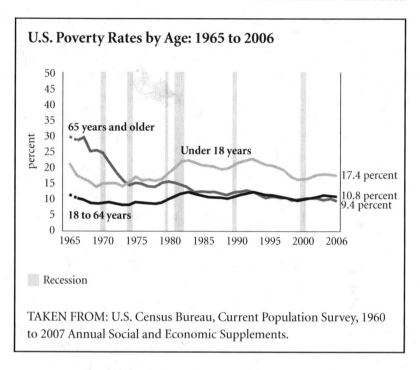

U.S. Poverty Rates by Age: 1965 to 2006

65 years and older

Under 18 years

17.4 percent

10.8 percent
9.4 percent

18 to 64 years

1965　1970　1975　1980　1985　1990　1995　2000　2006

Recession

TAKEN FROM: U.S. Census Bureau, Current Population Survey, 1960 to 2007 Annual Social and Economic Supplements.

Charles Murray took this further and discussed the concept of a dependency culture. He suggested that individuals are dependent on the state for benefits in order to live and do not seek employment. He suggested that the creation of a welfare state has led to the development of a subculture which undermines self belief, personal ambition and drive.

If individuals are responsible for their own poverty, and we take the stance that poverty is child abuse, then the family can be said to be abusing their child by allowing him/her to live in poverty. There are problems with this conclusion: if the child is living in poverty then by definition the family is also living in poverty. Since all members of the family are in the same position and suffering the same problems, are they too being abused? The difference may be that children have no way of improving their living conditions or of generating an income, whereas an adult may have.

Poverty Is Caused by Society

There are those who disagree that poverty is self induced and suggest that it is induced by society. The systems and forces that exist within society, which are produced and reproduced, induce poverty. Ethnicity, class and occupation, for example, will all influence resource allocation and distribution. Those who subscribe to this idea suggest that the lack of ambition among the poorer members of society is a consequence of poverty, not a cause. If this view is taken, society is not only causing poverty but is also harming the child. This conclusion also has problems.

If society causes the poverty and then goes on to try and solve it, can society dictate how the child and family should behave? For example, if a family is receiving benefits, society may take the view that it should decide how the money is spent. Parents may not appear to act in a way that is in the best interests of their children, or in a way that is viewed as appropriate by professionals. We may be quick to condemn a mother who spends her benefits or allowances on designer clothes for her children when the money was allocated for furniture. However, it is important to look at the more complex issues that may be arising in this situation. The mother in this case may be trying to avoid social exclusion and bring about a sense of belonging for herself and her child. *Measuring Child Poverty* endorses feeling accepted by society: being accepted in her neighbourhood may be more important to the mother than having a new table. Those who are not dependent on benefits can spend their money as they wish: so why should it be different when a family is living in poverty?

Neither of these explanations are conclusive and this article does not aim to find a definitive answer to what or who causes poverty. However, it is important to recognise that poverty is a complex issue and that it has profound effects on children and their families.

Links Between Poverty and Abuse

A child living in poverty may be without adequate food, shelter, clothing, protection and love. While they may not initially suffer actual physical harm, there is no doubt that harm is being caused and that living in this way will be detrimental to a child's wellbeing. Although love can be provided whatever a family's circumstances, it is only one part of a child's needs. Using the categories of abuse in the DH definition, poverty could be classed as a form of neglect. [According to the DH,] neglect is 'The persistent failure to meet a child's basic physical and/or psychological needs, likely to result in the serious impairment of the child's health or well being'. [C.] Beckett suggests that emotional abuse underlies most other forms of abuse and may include isolating a child in some way, or preventing him from socialising with peers, resulting in the child being stigmatised and/or isolated. Research by [R.] Oates *et al* suggested that neglected children seemed to be lower in self esteem than children who had been physically abused. Children suffering from neglect and emotional abuse have also been found to underachieve in school with significant implications for the rest of the child's life.

Classifying Poverty as Abuse

In 2001 there were 14.8 million children living in the UK. The number of children living in households below 60 per cent of median income was 3.8 million, 26 per cent of all children. Poverty can have significant effects on the health and education attainment of the child in the short and long term beginning at birth; there are more low birth weight babies born in deprived areas than in less deprived areas.

While there can be no denying that child poverty is a significant problem, deciding whether poverty constitutes child abuse is more difficult. If it is classed as abuse, then alleviating child poverty would have an even higher priority. Healthcare professionals would have to make it a priority to recognise child poverty in their clients and act accordingly. The Children Act includes a duty to recognise poverty, provide help and support to families—including making appropriate referrals—and recognise at-risk groups such as families from ethnic minorities, the unemployed and asylum seekers. Health promotion and education are a part of the health professional's response. [Judith A.] Oulton suggests that nurses must be educated to determine health needs and work towards empowering individuals to work with communities and vulnerable groups to address their unique needs. This is no easy task and providing appropriate interventions to support families living in poverty is not straightforward. Government initiatives such as Sure Start are helping by supporting family members to go back to work and developing direct services in a disadvantaged areas.

Abuse Statistics

If child poverty was classed as abuse then statistics recording the incidence of abuse would rise considerably. Under section 47 of the Children Act local authorities have a statutory duty to make enquiries when there is reasonable cause to suspect that any child is suffering or likely to suffer from significant harm. In England between 1999 and 2000 there were 160,000 such enquiries. A total of 19 per cent of referred children were placed on the child protection register and most were categorised under 'neglect'. Based on available statistics, of the children seen on a typical paediatric ward, 26 per cent will live in poverty and two in every 100 (0.02 per cent) will be on the child protection register. If child poverty was seen as abuse then the number of children who would be classed as being abused would increase from less than 1 per cent to around 26 per cent.

Action Is Necessary

One in four children in the UK is living in poverty. Tackling poverty may be high on the political agenda but eradicating it is not going to be straightforward. The causes of poverty are complex and continue to be debated. Is it caused by lack of motivation and unwillingness of parents and carers to improve their standard of living? If so, the resulting harm caused to the child is the fault of parents and carers. However, if the cause of poverty lies with society as a whole and the rules and regulations governing it, responsibility must lie there. What is clear is that action has to be taken to protect and provide for children so that their individual needs are met. Local authorities and healthcare professionals have a statutory duty to protect children. This duty already requires that child poverty is recognised and alleviated to ensure adequate care is given and the child enabled to grow and develop normally.

The definitions of child abuse and child poverty are closely related and it could be concluded that child poverty is indeed child abuse. Whether this would alter the priorities of health and social care professionals and lead to more work to eradicate poverty is debatable. The government is sending out the message that child poverty does exist and that steps must be taken to alleviate it: whether this massive task will be successful remains to be seen.

Periodical Bibliography

The following articles have been selected to supplement the diverse views presented in this chapter.

Associated Press   "Sect Minor Gives Birth to Boy," *MSNBC.com*, April 29, 2008.

Chuck Colson   "Is Religion Child Abuse: What About the Children?" *Christian Post*, October 11, 2007. www.christianpost.com/article/20071011/ is-religion-child-abuse.htm.

Susan Estrich   "California Spanking Ban Would Help Stop Child Abuse," *Fox News*, January 28, 2008. www.foxnews.com/story/0,2933,247902,00.html.

Christopher B. Fuselier   "Corporal Punishment of Children: California's Attempt and Inevitable Failure to Ban Spanking in the Home," *Journal of Juvenile Law*, vol. 28, 2007, pp. 82–99.

Nancy Gibbs   "The Polygamy Paradox," *Time*, October 1, 2007.

Mark S. Kiselica and Mandy Morrill-Richards   "Sibling Maltreatment: The Forgotten Abuse," *Journal of Counseling & Development*, vol. 85, Spring 2007, pp. 148–60.

Gretel C. Kovach   "Court Files Detail Claims of Sect's 'Pattern' of Abuse," *The New York Times*, April 9, 2008.

Ken MacQueen   "Polygamy: Legal in Canada," *Maclean's*, June 25, 2007.

Adam Nossiter   "In Alabama, a Crackdown on Pregnant Drug Users," *The New York Times*, March 15, 2008. www.nytimes.com/2008/03/15/us/ 15mothers.html.

Sureshrani Paintal   "Banning Corporal Punishment of Children: An Association for Cultural Economics International Position Paper," *Childhood Education*, vol. 83, no. 6, August 15, 2007, pp. 410–13.

OPPOSING
VIEWPOINTS®
SERIES

CHAPTER 2

What Causes Child Abuse?

Chapter Preface

A forty-year-old teacher, with no prior history of pedophilia, one day begins collecting child pornography. Increasingly, he faces stronger urges to act upon his new interest. Eventually he is kicked out of his home by his wife for making subtle sexual advances toward his step-daughter. He finds it impossible to follow a twelve-step program to help him fight his urges. His condition worsens. Distraught and suicidal, he takes himself to a hospital emergency room. He is afraid that he is going to rape his landlady, and he has a crippling headache. At the hospital, he propositions or leers at every female that he sees and is unaware that he has urinated all over himself.

A hospital psychiatrist finds that the man has balance problems and cannot copy words or pictures. An MRI reveals an egg-sized brain tumor pressing on his right frontal lobe. After the tumor is removed, his headache, balance problems, and confusion disappear—and so do his inappropriate sexual compulsions. In fact, he returns to his former self and eventually moves back in with his wife and step-daughter. He is profoundly relieved that he is not destined to be the evil monster that he felt he had turned into. Seven months later, however, he starts collecting pornography again. Another MRI reveals that the tumor has started to grow back, but again, when it is surgically removed, the urges disappear.

According to specialists, the man's condition made biological sense because the part of the brain affected by the tumor is the part of the brain that controls impulses. Although the tumor did not create the impulses, it made it very difficult for the man to put the brakes on his behavior. With the tumor, that part of his brain simply was not functioning.

While the man's medical condition is extremely rare, this case supports the theory that brain disorders can cause sociopathic behavior. In fact, brain tumors have been linked to other criminal activity, including murder. In 1966, from the bell tower at the University of Texas, Charles Whitman shot and killed fourteen students shortly after having killed his wife and mother. He was shot and killed by police. In his suicide note, Whitman had requested an autopsy, which revealed a brain tumor in his amygdala, a part of the brain that regulates emotional reactions.

Scientifically significant correlations between violence and brain damage also have been established. In a 1997 study, Dr. Monte Buchsbaum performed positron emission tomography (PET) scans on forty-four people, twenty-two of whom were facing murder charges and twenty-two otherwise similar people who did not have a history of violence. The scans revealed a significant correlation between violence and lower activity in areas of the brain that inhibit aggression.

In November 2007, study results were released that support the possibility that faulty brain wiring can cause pedophilia. Through computer analysis of magnetic resonance imaging (MRI) of the brains of more than 120 men, researchers found that the subset of pedophiles had much less white matter in their brains than did another subset of criminals whose crimes were not sex related. White matter is the tissue that connects various parts of the brain and carries nerve impulses. This research team previously found brain-related links to pedophilia in studies that suggested that pedophiles have lower IQs and that they are three times as likely to be left-handed.

According to the lead scientist of the study, these findings do not mean that pedophiles are not responsible for their actions. The studies do, however, provide a possible biological explanation for at least some cases of pedophilia, and the research calls into question the theory that pedophilia is primarily the result of childhood abuse.

As the viewpoints in this chapter illustrate, the debate over what causes pedophilia and other forms of child abuse is far from over.

> "There are certain risk factors and reci-
> pes for child abuse, and they include
> having an adult in the home who has
> poor bonding with the child."

Broken Homes Increase the Risk of Child Abuse

Jill King Greenwood

Fewer children live with both biological parents now than did decades ago, resulting in more and more children living with and being taken care of by adults who are not bonded with them, particularly boyfriends of mothers. Such situations put small children in danger, according to this viewpoint, which cites statistics and presents recent cases of children who were killed by their mothers' boyfriends. Jill King Greenwood is a reporter for The Pittsburgh Tribune-Review.

As you read, consider the following questions:

1. What percentage of families with children are one-parent families, according to the U.S. Census Bureau?

2. How much higher is the likelihood that children living with unrelated adults will die of child abuse than children living with two biological parents?

3. What two reasons does the author offer for single mothers not taking advantage of free quality childcare provided by federal funding?

Experts say it's a troubling trend: men accused of killing children of the women they live with.

As more American children grow up in homes without their two biological parents, the risk of child abuse is markedly higher than in traditional nuclear family structures, they say.

In the past 12 months [2007], four children in Southwestern Pennsylvania ages 14 months and younger allegedly have been abused and later died, and police have arrested the boyfriends of their mothers:

- A North Versailles man watching his girlfriend's 14-month-old boy put the baby's head in the crook of his arm in June and squeezed until he "heard a popping noise," killing the child at her White Oak home, police said.

- A 10-month-old Troy Hill girl was sexually assaulted and fatally beaten, and police arrested her mother's live-in boyfriend, who was babysitting.

- A Butler County man is charged with beating his girlfriend's 13-month-old son to death in June after he found out he was not the boy's father.

- In March, a 3-month-old Fayette County girl died as a result of severe skull fractures, and investigators charged the infant's mother's boyfriend with aggravated assault. Officials are awaiting the opinion of another pathologist before deciding whether to charge James Ray Morrison, 27, with homicide.

"There are certain risk factors and recipes for child abuse, and they include having an adult in the home who has poor bonding with the child," said Dr. Janet Squires, chief of the Child Advocacy Center at Children's Hospital of Pittsburgh.

"Other Men's Children"

"They may be in the relationship for the mother and not have much interest in the child and view them as an annoyance. These are men raising other men's children, and though there are exceptions, they don't all necessarily want to do it."

In the latest case of a child's death, Clinton Smith, 30, is scheduled to appear Nov. 30 [2007] in Pittsburgh Municipal Court on charges of homicide, rape, aggravated assault and other offenses. Police say he beat and sexually assaulted Da'Niyah Marie Jackson, 10 months, at her Troy Hill home while her mother, LaToya Jackson, was working an 11-hour shift as a waitress.

She returned home to find her baby—whom family members described as content and not prone to crying or fussing—bruised, beaten and unresponsive. The girl died two days later at Children's Hospital.

In another case, a 7-year-old North Side girl was beaten and burned more than 37 times with cigarettes in November 2006. Police charged her uncle, who was living with the family and babysitting the first-grader and her siblings when the injuries happened.

No Clear Statistics

The existing data on child abuse in America is patchwork, making it difficult to track national trends. The most recent federal survey on child maltreatment, compiled for the U.S. Department of Health and Human Services, is from 2005 and tracks nearly 900,000 abuse reports to state agencies. The survey did not examine how rates of abuse correlate with parents' marital status or the makeup of a child's household.

Fatherhood Facts

- 24 million children (34 percent) live absent their biological father.

- Nearly 20 million children (27 percent) live in single-parent homes.

- Over 3.3 million children live with an unmarried parent and the parent's cohabiting partner.

- Children who live absent their biological fathers are, on average, at least two to three times more likely to be poor, to use drugs, to experience educational, health, emotional and behavioral problems, to be victims of child abuse, and to engage in criminal behavior than their peers who live with their married, biological (or adoptive) parents.

- Children with involved, loving fathers are significantly more likely to do well in school, have healthy self-esteem, exhibit empathy and pro-social behavior, and avoid high-risk behaviors such as drug use, truancy, and criminal activity compared to children who have uninvolved fathers.

- Studies on parent-child relationships and child well-being show that father love is an important factor in predicting the social, emotional, and cognitive development and functioning of children and young adults.

http://www.fatherhood.gov/statistics/index.cfm;
http.//www/fatherhood.org/fatherfacts/.

Similarly, data on the roughly 1,500 child-abuse fatalities that occur annually in the United States leave unanswered questions. Many of those deaths result from parental neglect, rather than physical abuse. Of the 500 or so deaths caused by physical abuse, the federal statistics do not specify how many were caused by a stepparent or unmarried partner of the parent.

Other studies reinforce the fears of experts that children from broken homes are at a higher risk of abuse:

- Children living in households with unrelated adults are nearly 50 times as likely to die of inflicted injuries as children living with two biological parents, according to a study of Missouri abuse reports published in the journal of the American Academy of Pediatrics in 2005.

- According to several studies from the University of New Hampshire's Crimes Against Children Research Center, children living in stepfamilies or with single parents are at higher risk of physical or sexual assault than children living with two biological or adoptive parents.

Fewer Biological Families

"This is the dark underbelly of cohabitation," said University of Virginia sociology professor Brad Wilcox. "Cohabitation has become quite common, and most people think, 'What's the harm?' The harm is we're increasing a pattern of relationships that's not good for children."

In the late 1970s, nearly 80 percent of America's children lived with both parents. Now, only two-thirds of them do, according to U.S. Census Bureau statistics. Of all families with children, nearly 29 percent are one-parent families, up from 17 percent in 1977, according to the U.S. Census Bureau.

The result is a marked rise in the likelihood that adults and children with no biological tie will reside together.

"I've seen many cases of physical and sexual abuse that come up with boyfriends, stepparents," said Eliana Gil, clinical director for the national abuse-prevention group Childhelp.

Dr. Mary Carrasco, director of A Child's Place at Mercy Hospital, Uptown, said she often sees abuse cases where a nonbiological man caring for another man's child felt competition for the mother's attention.

"There's often a jealousy issue," Carrasco said. "And to some men, the fact that they're at home, changing diapers and comforting a child while the woman is working causes resentment. It's a threat to their manhood."

An Unfortunate Situation

Squires said many single mothers find themselves in an almost impossible predicament: With little education or job training, they work jobs paying minimum wage and cannot afford quality child care.

"Sometimes women get into these relationships with live-in boyfriends for emotional or financial need," Squires said. "Often when we see cases of a child being abused by a mother's boyfriend, it's when the mother was out working long hours and the child was left at home with an adult male who isn't working and doesn't care too much for that child.

"Some people can blame the mothers and say they shouldn't have had children until they were financially ready to raise them, but it's the children who are caught in the middle and the children who suffer."

A *Tribune-Review* sampling of about a dozen child care centers in Allegheny County showed that full-time care for a child 6 weeks to 5 years old ranges from about $450 a month to nearly $1,000.

An Inadequate Solution

Some programs subsidize the cost based on the parent's income, and federally funded programs such as Head Start and Early Head Start exist for child care and preschool programs. But experts warn that some programs have long waiting lists for enrollment and don't provide services at night and on weekends, when many single mothers find themselves working long shifts at menial jobs.

The Allegheny County Department of Human Services has programs designed to prevent and educate parents and caregivers about child abuse, said Leslie Reicher, an administrator in the unit of outreach and prevention. One is First Steps, which provides home visits in McKeesport, the Hill District, South Side and North Side to assist pregnant women and families with children younger than 6, Reicher said.

Preventing and stopping child abuse—regardless of who is living in a home with a child—is everyone's responsibility, Squires said.

"If we, as a society, truly valued and treasured our children, we would think twice about who we leave them with and would do everything we could to protect them," she said. "Otherwise, the children are the ones who, ultimately, pay the price."

> "It is not easy to spend weeks and months shooting and killing others, and then turn off all of these violent tendencies after coming home."

Military Deployment Increases the Risk of Child Abuse

Paul J. Fink

This viewpoint examines problems that arise in families due to military deployment. Deployment itself puts stress on the parent left home to care for the kids and everything else, and that stress and other factors increase the chance that the parent, mothers especially, will abuse the children. In addition, when parents return from active duty, they may have difficulty suddenly switching from military life with combat and direct orders to life at home being parents, especially if they suffer from post-traumatic stress disorder. Paul J. Fink is a psychiatrist, a consultant, and professor of psychiatry at Temple University in Pennsylvania.

As you read, consider the following questions:

1. What three things predicted child abuse by mothers in families where the father was deployed, according to one study?

2. Posttraumatic stress disorder increases the tendency of what behaviors, according to the author?

3. What examples of the erosion of social values does the author give?

Rarely do we think about how stressful it is for soldiers' wives who are left behind when their husbands are deployed. The spouse must take on all of the responsibilities that formerly had been handled by both parents. In addition, in most cases, the mother is now totally responsible for all discipline and, in the event that she was the comforter of the children when her husband was the disciplinarian, she might have difficulty switching roles.

Therefore, she might become more rigid and "violent" than she might have been had her soldier husband stayed home.

Such switches in roles also are very hard on the children, who might be accustomed to mom as the soft parent. As a result, the children sometimes become more difficult to control than they are with dad, whose role as the tougher disciplinarian was well understood. This change in family dynamics can exacerbate the children's negative behaviors and mom's exasperation with the children. Yet, this is only one of the wife's frustrations and stressors.

Multiple Stressors

Sexual deprivation also can become a factor. One day her man is at home; the next day he is gone. The greatest problem must be the wife's sense of aloneness, which also might be connected to loneliness.

For those women who had been the more dependent partner to be thrust into control of the house, the money, and the children, many new stressors are added into the equation. Much depends on the predeployment division of labor in the family and the amount of social interaction to which she had grown accustomed before the deployment.

One study that examined these issues in military families found distinct differences between the genders in child abuse potential. The study of 175 fathers (93% active duty) and 590 mothers (16% active duty) in a home visitation program sponsored by the Army found that the unique predictors for child physical abuse potential for mothers included marital dissatisfaction, low social support, and low family cohesion. The only unique predictor found for fathers was low family expressiveness.

Stressed Fathers

Despite the findings of the JAMA [Journal of the American Medical Association] study showing higher rates of child abuse among civilian wives because of added stressors, we also need to remember that the stressors on military men also are heightened.

The Army's desire to redeploy young enlisted men three and four times to Iraq or Afghanistan can prove devastating to both the soldier and his wife—and to the entire family, for that matter. The threat of injury or death is increased, and the wife might not be as "patriotic" as her husband, so she might be less enthusiastic than he about his returning again and again to the combat area.

Furthermore, the more combat he sees, the more likely he is to develop posttraumatic stress disorder (PTSD) or acute stress disorder (ASD) which can be a motivator for his own increasing negative behavior toward his children. It needs to be clear to a psychiatrist that children's vulnerability to being treated badly is increased whenever life's circumstances change—and war does terrible things to people.

For enlisted soldiers, stress is very high. They have to follow orders, join in the common belief regarding their purpose in fighting the war, and endure an increasing number of horrors—especially the loss of friends and companions.

A Setup for Violence

They also acquire a greater propensity for violence. It is not easy to spend weeks and months shooting and killing others, and then turn off all of these violent tendencies after coming home—and act with sweetness and kindness toward the children and spouses in a single day.

Furthermore, PTSD increases this tendency toward rage, impulsivity, acting out, shouting, hitting, and even indiscreet sexual behavior. Often, these soldiers are young, unsophisticated, and given to excessive behavior even before being deployed to combat for the first time.

As we think about the horrors of war, we rarely delve psychoanalytically into the ravaging effects on the psyche of war, stress, and change. Here, I am examining just a few of the possible variations and permutations that are related to the deployment of young people to war zones. However, it is clear to me that it is incumbent upon us to try to understand what is happening in these families beyond just counting the number of incidents.

For example, evidence shows that military families in general have more family violence than does the average American family. In addition, it is important to look for causality whenever we learn about violent behavior in adolescents, the public in general, or the increasing use of guns in our society.

Changing Social Values

It is time for us to rethink our social values. I believe that the increasing influence of religion in this country is growing out of a real fear coming not only from the increasing violence in our society, but from many of the factors antecedent to the rise of negative behavior.

The incredible erosion of common courtesy; the trashing of societal behaviors of kindness, thoughtfulness, and respect for the elderly; the acceptance of vile language as part of ev-

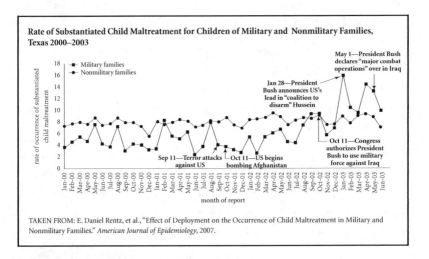

Rate of Substantiated Child Maltreatment for Children of Military and Nonmilitary Families, Texas 2000–2003

TAKEN FROM: E. Daniel Rentz, et al., "Effect of Deployment on the Occurrence of Child Maltreatment in Military and Nonmilitary Families." *American Journal of Epidemiology*, 2007.

eryday discourse; and the sharing of private information on cell phones—regardless of who can hear it—are examples of this erosion.

Such changes in the culture have been very destructive to society and very instructive to young people who believe that "anything goes."

A Violent Culture

In addition, easy access to pornography, and the constant use of violence as entertainment in movies, on the Internet, and in electronic games for children from 3 to 33 hours a day, have had a negative impact on our social values systems. America's love affair with guns is essentially wiping out a large number of our youth nationwide, and it is almost totally disregarded by our legislators and by most men on the street.

When an entire generation of our youth has been schooled in violence, we can begin to understand the premise upon which both the current wars in the Middle East and the war on our streets is predicated. In war, soldiers have permission to act out violently. We are horrified when they act out violently against innocent civilians or they act sadistically against helpless prisoners. It is not much of a jump to go from prisoners under your control to children under your control. The impulses toward cruelty and harming others are the basic un-conscious reality that these soldiers learn in the Middle East, and many take those impulses home to Middle America.

Orders from the Top

In addition to the evidence I mentioned earlier about violence in military families, there is some evidence that men in the armed forces tend to do more abuse to children than do men in the general population. All of the armed forces are top down. Those at the top give the orders; those at the bottom follow the orders.

I have had several patients whose fathers were noncom-missioned officers (NCOs) at the staff sergeant level. Their sons characterized them as martinets who terrified their sons by their uniforms, stiff backs, and propensity to punish.

When these patients heard their fathers' footsteps coming into the home, they were terrorized.

Whether physical punishment took place or not, or re-gardless of whether humiliation of the son by the father took place, it was clear to me in those cases that the father brought his behaviors from the barracks to the home. Often the recruit and the son were interchangeable in the father's mind. So it should not surprise us to learn that men in the military are harsher to their wives and children than is the average guy on the street.

This takes us full circle to the role of wives while husbands are deployed. Particularly for wives who have been excessively controlled and dominated, the sudden freedom and essential release from bondage can be exhilarating and frightening, and their subsequent abuse of their children can be fraught with guilt and depression.

Unique Families

Psychiatry must develop a whole new set of skills to under-stand, and, where necessary, intervene in the families of sol-diers where domestic violence or child abuse takes place.

Members of the armed services are unique in both their beliefs and behaviors. It is a big mistake to generalize them as exactly as we would civilians. Thousands of soldiers are returning from Iraq and Afghanistan with physical disabilities and emotional impairments. Whether they have an amputated leg or arm or PTSD or other psychiatric disorders such as anxiety or depression, everyone in the family suffers.

An embittered, angry father changes the family dynamics extensively. A disabled father, no longer able to be a breadwinner, feels castrated, and acts horribly and violently to cover up inner feelings of being "a broken man."

A Family Matter

If we as psychiatrists treat only the injured soldier, we make a terrible mistake. The soldier may come to therapy blaming everyone around him and may be unable to recognize his own suffering, crushed masculinity, sense of hopelessness and worthlessness, and movement from total control to complete dependency. The JAMA article concentrates on the number of incidents of child abuse by soldiers and their wives, but it does not look at the destruction of the family that occurs as a result of deployment; how deployment affects the wives; or the effects of combat itself on the soldiers.

We as a profession have an enormous responsibility to be an active combatant in these wars and to try to salvage what we can of these broken and damaged families.

Clearly, family therapy may be essential. A 12-year-old who feels he has lost one or both parents enters his adolescence with one arm tied behind him. Just when this child needs a competent family to guide him through the next 5 years, the child is bereft.

Individual therapy, cognitive-behavioral therapy, or psychodynamic therapy may be necessary for one or both parents, and couples therapy may work best in all cases.

A Comprehensive Plan

A careful assessment of the situation and a willingness to do the evaluation with a full understanding of the impact of war on the family—both before and afterward—would be an important tool for the therapist.

Providing adequate pharmacologic intervention for wives in distress when their husbands are deployed, and certainly for those soldiers coming home damaged and hurt, is another important aspect of our role.

Finally, it is vital that we do some preventive work with these families. "Forewarned is forearmed"—helping these men and women understand some of these variables at the outset—would help avert some of the sequelae [consequences].

The number of casualties—the men, their wives, and their children—of war is astronomical, and I believe psychiatry has an important role to play.

> "The Internet has become for pedophiles the greatest empowering tool ever created."

The Internet Fosters Child Pornography and Child Abuse

Brian Bethune

While pedophilia is nothing new, the Internet has affected how child predators operate. According to this viewpoint the Internet makes it easier for pedophiles to find and support each other, find victims, and draw others into their web. This viewpoint also disputes two common myths about child pornography: that looking at it is harmless and that while the victims are underage, they are already sexualized. Brian Bethune writes for Maclean's, a weekly Canadian news magazine.

As you read, consider the following questions:

1. According to the National Center for Missing and Exploited Children, what percentage of seized child pornography was photographed by children themselves who had been talked into it by "friends" that they had met on the Internet?

2. What does journalist Julian Sher, author of *One Child at a Time*, consider to be the most important myth that he wants to dispel with his book?

3. What percentage of known victims of child predators are younger than five years old?

In Britain, London police once arrested a photographer with 130,000 pornographic images of children. That was in 1874, a striking reminder from investigative journalist Julian Sher in his *One Child at a Time* that there have always been pedophiles among us. Sher's riveting account of online predators and their police pursuers also cites a famous survey of 200 male undergraduates in California in which one in five admitted to some kind of sexual attraction to small children, while almost one in 10 reported having sexual fantasies about them. Seven per cent said they might even have sex with a child if they could avoid detection and punishment. In Canada, Dr. John Bradford of the Royal Ottawa Hospital's Sexual Behaviours Clinic estimates that two to seven per cent of the population could have pedophiliac tendencies.

Pedophiles are thus scattered across society: well off or poor, tortured with guilt or enthusiastic participants, involved in functioning sexual relationships with other adults or complete loners. Their prevalence means that up to 20 per cent of adults were molested as children in some manner. And not by strangers: up to 90 per cent of victims suffer at the hands of relatives or others they know well.

The Role of the Internet

For all we don't know about pedophilia, though, there is one evermore manifest fact. Just as it has proved for millions of ordinary people, the Internet has become for pedophiles the greatest empowering tool ever created. Which means, according to Sher, that what has always been part of the human condition is now growing exponentially worse, "both in magnitude and in severity."

Disturbing Statistics

100,000 Web sites offering child pornography
(U.S. Customs Service and TopTenREVIEWS, 2004)

79% of teens state that they aren't careful enough when giving out information about themselves online
(Pew Internet and Amercian Life, "Protecting Teens Online," 2005)

64% of teens say that they do things online that they wouldn't want their parents to know about
(Pew Internet and American Life, "Protecting Teens Online," 2005)

$3 billion Child pornography revenue annually
(TopTenREVIEWS, 2004)

1 in 5 Children are sexually solicited online
(only 25% of those told a parent)
(Online Victimization, David Finkelher, 2000)

89% Sexual solicitations occurred in either chat rooms or Instant Messaging
(Online Victimization, David Finkelher, 2000)

TAKEN FROM: Child Predator Unit and Operation SAFESURF, Pennsylvania Attorney General, Tom Corbett, "Cybersafety: Protecting Your Kids and Teens Online."

The Internet "doesn't create pedophilia," Sher notes, "but it certainly does fuel it." In the past, pedophiles were isolated, repressed by the revulsion most people felt toward them and limited in their opportunities. "But now offender after offender will tell you about their eureka moment," says Sher, "when they first went online and saw not only the images— the *live* images—available, but immersed themselves in the acceptance, the assurance they were among like-minded people."

The Temptation of Big Money

The Net has vastly increased the money-making possibilities of child pornography, and hence the supply on offer. In the late 1990s, Thomas and Janice Reedy, a Dallas couple who never earned enough to own a home, were parking his and hers Mercedes in their mansion driveway. Their money came from Landslide, an Internet portal that offered credit-card customers access to 5,000 porn sites. Business limped along at first, Thomas Reedy later confessed, until he realized where the real money was. In the first month of offering access to a site called Child Rape, the Reedys garnered 1,277 registrations, and over the next two years Landslide brought in more than $10 million.

Unwitting Participation

More insidiously, the Internet doesn't just make access easier, it facilitates supply: the Washington-based National Center for Missing and Exploited Children [NCMEC] now finds that as much as 10 per cent of their seized material comes from older children who have taken compromising pictures of themselves. More often than not these self-made images were the result of what NCMEC calls "online enticement"—children manipulated by a "friend" met on the Web who coaxed them into snapping pictures of their own bodies. In a U.S. Justice Department survey, one in seven young Web surfers reported encountering unwanted sexual material or online harassment.

"Not Just Pictures"

Worst of all, adds Sher, "the Internet drags in those who probably wouldn't have done what they did otherwise." Canadians will need no further reminder of that than the case of Michael Briere. In his confession to the rape and murder of 10-year-old Holly Jones, Briere told the court he had fantasized about molesting a girl for "maybe a year or two." He kept alive what he called his "dark secret" on the Web: "The more I saw it, the more I longed for it in my heart." On the night of May 12, 2003, "I viewed some material beforehand. I just got excited. I really wanted to do it. I really wanted to have sex with a child. I just came out of my place and she was just there." Forty minutes later Holly was dead.

Briere's tipping point goes to the first and, to Sher, most important myth he wants to dispel with his book. "It's not *just* pictures," Sher says emphatically. "They're crime-scene photos. But you still hear from people that 'Better perverts look at dirty pictures than actually molest a child.' Looking doesn't deter doing; study after study shows that 35 to 40 percent of those arrested for pornography possession are also hands-on abusers." Another common misconception, according to Sher, is that many of the victims are already sexual beings—under-aged only by law. In fact, fully 39 per cent of known victims, according to NCMEC, are only 5 or younger; 19 per cent are under 3.

Unknown Causes

We still don't know much about the men and most are men, although a tenth are women—responsible for this spiral of abuse, especially what we really wart to know: the combination of brain chemistry, genetics and personal experience that makes them what they are. The nature vs. nurture argument, as so often, rages inconclusively around them. Much points to a hard-wired nature: Sher cites British psychologist Joe Sullivan, who found that 80 per cent of offenders knew by age 18 that they were sexually attracted to children. On the other hand, 33 per cent of offenders were abused themselves as children, a rate statistically higher than the general population—fodder for the nurture side. Whatever the cause, the condition is incurable. "They know it doesn't go away," Sullivan says. "Once you've got it, you've got it."

| "When the sexual abuse of students by educators involves digital technology, the harm can be heightened in ways that make an already damaging betrayal of trust even more devastating."

The Internet Fosters Child Sexual Abuse by Educators

Lesli A. Maxwell

Inappropriate relationships and sexual relations between school staff and students are not new problems. However, our everyday digital technology makes it easier for students and staff to start and maintain secret relationships. This viewpoint presents cases of such relationships, the need for clearer policies and better preventative advice for new teachers, and discusses the fact that the same digital technology makes it easier to identify and successfully prosecute the adults in these cases. Lesli A. Maxwell writes for Education Week *on various topics, including urban education and school safety.*

As you read, consider the following questions:

1. What three social networking tools are mentioned in this article?

Lesli A. Maxwell, "Digital Age Adds New Dimension To Incidents of Staff-Student Sex," *Education Week*, vol. 27, November 28, 2007, pp. 1, 14. Copyright © 2007 Editorial Projects in Education. Reproduced by permission.

2. What do the generation of younger teachers have a different concept of, and how can this different concept lead to inappropriate relationships with students?

3. To prosecutors, what are the advantages of digital technology in cases of staff-student sex?

The 44-year-old guidance counselor would send text messages to the 15-year-old boy on the boy's cellphone in the middle of the school day. But the messages had nothing to do with academics or counseling. With words along the lines of "see u soon" and "how about now?," the female counselor would then arrange to get the boy a pass to leave class and come to her office. Sometimes, she and the student would have sexual contact in her office. Other times, she took him off campus to have sex.

"Text messaging actually made it much easier for the liaisons to take place," said Mary Jo McGrath, an education lawyer in Santa Barbara, Calif., who testified as an expert witness for the boy's family in their lawsuit against the New Jersey school district where he was a freshman in high school.

The counselor's typed text messages to arrange trysts are the sort of digital come-ons that experts say have become a new and prevalent feature in cases that involve educators accused of sexually abusing students. Increasingly, those who follow such cases say, teachers and other school employees who prey on students are using the current must-have tools of adolescent social networks—cellphone text messaging, Web sites such as MySpace and Facebook, and e-mail—to foster inappropriate relationships and perpetrate abuse.

"This is most definitely an emerging trend that school districts and school leaders may not have on their radar screens, but they should," said Robert J. Shoop, the director of the Cargill Center for Ethical Leadership at Kansas State University and the author of a book on how school districts can identify and deal with sexual misconduct by educators.

When the sexual abuse of students by educators involves digital technology, the harm can be heightened in ways that make an already damaging betrayal of trust even more devastating. Abusers can use the Internet, e-mail, or text messaging, for example, to constantly pursue students, in and out of school. In some extreme cases, they may use the Web in a way that magnifies the abuse exponentially, as a 6th grade teacher in Vermont did recently when he was charged with using his students as models for his homemade child pornography.

At the same time, the electronic trail left by such communications can present evidence for authorities investigating allegations of educator misconduct. For some officials, that trail has become an invaluable tool in rooting out bad actors even when they don't have a cooperating victim.

Clear Policy Advised

For school leaders, the widespread use of such digital communications between teachers and students presents a new complication to the delicate management of relationships between school employees and students.

Some cases are clearly inappropriate and raise obvious red flags, like the teacher investigated in one state recently who was sending text messages to his student in the middle of the night. But what about the teacher in another state who had a MySpace page filled with photos and personal information who shares a link to her page with a student?

"The intimacy that these communications can create, and the blurring of boundaries, are a real danger because it can seem so innocent, and so contemporary," Mr. Shoop said. "But every school should have a very clear policy on what is appropriate use of technology for teachers and school staff."

In the East Greenbush Central School District in Rensselaer County, N.Y., an ongoing case has prompted district officials to think about how to address the issue with school staff members.

A 37-year-old high school teacher in the 5,000-student district was sentenced this month to nine months behind bars and 10 years' probation after admitting to having oral sex in his classroom with a 16-year-old male student.

During the investigation, police found that the teacher, Kirk James Hellwig, had been posing as a 15-year-old boy named "Kirk" on a MySpace page he had created. Authorities said that the teacher's MySpace page was not directly connected to the abuse case.

Mr. Hellwig, who was a social studies teacher, also pleaded guilty to using indecent material to converse with the victim online and will serve 10 years' probation for that charge. He was ordered to permanently surrender his teaching license and resign from the East Greenbush district.

Case Spurs Outreach

Rebecca Furlong, who became the superintendent of the district in August, declined to discuss the details of the case. But she said the role of the Internet and MySpace had raised her awareness about the need to look more closely at what types of communication between teachers and students are appropriate.

"We are looking at incorporating these issues of how teachers communicate with their students and what is appropriate into future professional development, as well as our mentoring program for new teachers," Ms. Furlong said. "Clearly, the use of the Web needs to become a vital piece of talking about what's appropriate."

In the wake of the incident, the district worked with a state senator to disseminate a computer program to all middle and high school parents to teach them and their children about social-networking sites such as MySpace and the potential dangers associated with them, Ms. Furlong said.

Effects on Targeted Students: Academic, Emotional and Developmental

Targets of educator sexual misconduct report that they suffer emotional, educational, and developmental or health effects.

At least a third of students report behaviors that would negatively affect academic achievement:

• Avoid the teacher or other educator (43 percent).

• Do not want to go to school (36 percent).

• Do not talk much in class (34 percent).

• Have trouble paying attention (31 percent).

• Stayed home from school or cut a class (29 percent).

• Found it hard to study (29 percent).

About a quarter of students who were targets of educator sexual misconduct report academic or discipline repercussions that they attribute to the incident.

• Thought about changing schools (19 percent).

• Changed schools (6 percent).

• Received a lower grade on a test or assignment (25 percent).

• Received a lower grade in a class (25 percent).

• Got into trouble with school authorities (25 percent).

• Felt less likely to get a good grade (23 percent).

U.S. Department of Education, Office of the Under Secretary,
Educator Sexual Misconduct: A Synthesis of Existing Literature,
Washington, D.C., 2004.

Many school administrators encourage teachers to communicate electronically with their students and parents on academic matters. Some even encourage teachers to create Web pages.

Mr. Shoop of Kansas State, who last month gave a keynote address to the National Association of State Directors of Teacher Education and Certification on the use of technology in cases of educator sexual exploitation, said that in districts with many young teachers, clear guidelines and frank discussions about how those electronic communications are to be used are especially critical.

"Many of the younger teachers coming into the profession are from a generation that has an entirely different concept of privacy and what professional boundaries are," he said. "We are talking about 22- and 23-year-old teachers who already have MySpace pages and Facebook pages."

That issue is of particular concern to state education officials who are responsible for judging what is and isn't appropriate.

"If you've got a young educator who is in a rock band in his private life and has a MySpace page with explicit lyrics on it—and his students find out about it—that is one thing," said Victoria Chamberlain the executive director of Oregon's Teacher Standards and Practices Commission and the current president of the National Association of State Directors of Teacher Education and Certification. "That's completely different than a teacher who has a Web site and walks down the hall at school saying to kids,—'Hey, hey, have you seen my Web site?'"

In Texas, where Doug D. Phillips directs the investigations of school staff misconduct for the state education agency, "almost all" the cases that involve allegations of sex abuse, he said, include digital communications via the Web or cellphones. "Suddenly an educator has all the opportunity in the world to have direct contact with a student outside the school setting," he said. "They don't have to call the home directly anymore and hang up when the parent answers. They can just send the kid a text message."

Ms. McGrath, the education lawyer, said most of the "grooming process" through which abusers gain students' trust still happens at school. But she said the technology has made it easier for predators to pursue their victims continually.

"They can get at them 24 hours a day if they want," she said. "And they use the technology in a way that makes them appear to be a peer to students."

Investigative Tool

At the same time, the widespread use of such digital communications has also helped bring some of the cases to light, and when investigated, often provides evidence for both state education authorities who must weigh whether to revoke an educator's license and law-enforcement authorities who may prosecute an offender in court.

In Vermont, for example, the mother of a 12-year-old boy discovered a naked photograph of her son attached to a text message on his cellphone earlier this year, said Mark Oettinger, the general counsel for the Vermont Department of Education.

The message and photo were allegedly sent by Richard A. Foster, a 6th grade teacher at the boy's elementary school in Bradford, Vt. The mother's discovery eventually led to state and federal charges against Mr. Foster, who is accused of molesting children and using some of his students as models in the manufacturing of homemade child pornography.

"These technological communications, in my mind, have provided a treasure trove of investigative material that better documents the inappropriate conduct of educators," said Bart Zabin, the principal investigator for the office of school personnel review and accountability in the New York state education department. "In the past, so many of these cases were hampered by one person's word against another person's, which made it very difficult for investigators."

Now, Mr. Zabin said, e-mail correspondence, cellphone records, and Internet communications have become a part of almost every investigation. They are particularly valuable, he said, in cases where the alleged victim will not talk to investigators.

"This kind of evidence has allowed us to establish wrongdoing in several cases even when we did not have a direct witness," he said. "In many ways, it's helping us root out people who might not otherwise have been [caught]."

That could have been the case with the high school guidance counselor in New Jersey. Ms. McGrath said the woman had been a teacher, and had been accused of inappropriate behavior toward a student during a school dance earlier in her career.

"The solution then was to take her out of the classroom and make her a counselor," Ms. McGrath said. This time, she said, the trail of text messages the counselor left helped prove that the abuse had taken place.

The counselor, who resigned quickly after the allegations surfaced, has paid some damages to the victim and struck a plea agreement with local prosecutors, Ms. McGrath said. The school district also agreed to pay the boy and his family a "hefty" sum, she said.

"But no amount of money can compensate him for the long-term effects this has had on him," Ms. McGrath said. "He, like so many others, felt he was in love and lost his— 'best friend' when the abuse came to light. To this day he grapples with whether the abuse was his fault, and he has lost his faith in people and in himself."

> "A number of studies performed over a period spanning more than half a century ... have shown that an extremely large percentage of sexually active homosexuals also participate in child sexual molestation."

Homosexual Men Are More Likely than Heterosexual Men to Sexually Abuse Boys

Brian W. Clowes and David L. Sonnier

The past several years have been marked by clergy sexual abuse scandals, particularly in the Roman Catholic Church. In this viewpoint Brian W. Clowes and David L. Sonnier react to activists who deny that the source of the problem may possibly be homosexual clergy. Citing many studies and quotations from active homosexuals and clergyman, they draw a link between homosexuality and sexual abuse. They conclude by saying that homosexuals should not necessarily be banned from the priesthood, but that all Catholic clergy be required to sign a statement of faith condemning all homosexual acts. Brian W. Clowes is a graduate of the U.S. Military Academy at West Point and he is

Brian W. Clowes and David L. Sonnier, "Child Molestation by Homosexuals and Heterosexuals," *Homiletic & Pastoral Review*, May 2005, pp. 44–54. Copyright © Ignatius Press, San Francisco. All rights reserved. Reproduced by permission.

the director of research and training for Human Life International. David L. Sonnier is an assistant professor of computer science at Lyon College in Batesville, Arkansas, and a doctoral student at the University of Arkansas, Little Rock.

As you read, consider the following questions:

1. What do the authors say is the only way to solve the problem of child molestation by clergy in the Catholic Church?
2. If most of the offending priests are not true pedophiles, then what are they, according to the John Jay study?
3. According to Clowes and Sonnier, the argument that "gays" are "born that way" is irrelevant. Why?

The [Catholic] Church has always had a small number of priests and other religious who have taken advantage of their positions of authority and influence in order to gain sexual favors or to take advantage of the helpless. The problem of clerical child sexual molestation, particularly in the United States, has been widely exposed and publicized over the last several years. The numerous recent revelations have exposed the problem as much deeper and more widespread than most would have previously believed.

During the current crisis, homosexual activists within and outside the Catholic Church have done everything they could to divert attention away from even the *possibility* that there may be a higher percentage of homosexuals among the priesthood than in the general public, and that this may be the root of the problem of child sexual molestation within the Church. It is particularly the link between homosexuality and child molestation that they seek to deny.

For example, Dignity USA kicked off its "Stop Blaming Gay Priests" campaign during the meeting of the United States Catholic Bishops Conference in Washington, D.C., November 10–13, 2002. The group said, "DigntyUSA [sic] is calling on the U.S. Catholic bishops to stop blaming gay priests for the clergy sexual abuse scandal. All credible evidence discounts any link between the molestation of children and homosexuality."

The situation has become so charged that anyone who even *suggests* that there may be a connection between homosexuality and pedophilia is instantly and reflexively labeled a "homophobe" and a "gay basher." The powerful homosexual lobby reacts instinctively to negative publicity and information by, as researcher Laird Wilcox calls it, "ritually defaming" those who dare raise their voices. Organized homosexual groups first attempt to completely ignore the evidence, or, if it simply cannot be ignored, they smear and discredit those who produced it.

Discussion Is Necessary

Such casual dismissal of documented facts, and the accompanying refusal to even *discuss* the possibility of a link between an active homosexual lifestyle and child sexual abuse, is a grave disservice not only to the victims, but also to society at large. Obviously, a proven link between homosexual orientation and child sexual molestation would badly damage the carefully crafted public relations image of the homosexual rights movement. Therefore, instead of calmly and rationally discussing the issues, homosexual rights leaders subscribe to the axiom "the best defense is a good [and loud] offense," and remain in a permanent attack mode.

The only way to solve the problem of priestly child molestation is to proceed methodically: establish the facts, objectively study all facts relating to the situation, and finally, but most importantly, have the courage and faith to respond by taking appropriate steps. If all of this is not done, any such effort, no matter how well intentioned or vigorously pursued, will be utterly squandered. Certainly we owe it to the victims—and to the Catholic Faith itself—to determine the truth behind this volatile topic.

Studies on the Frequency of Homosexual-Child Molestation

Dignity USA and other homosexual groups strenuously deny any connection whatever between a homosexual orientation and child sexual molestation. They repeatedly claim, as Dignity USA does, that "All credible evidence discounts any link between the molestation of children and homosexuality."

Yet these groups never cite any of this "credible evidence," nor do they quote any studies to buttress their claims that there is no such connection.

In fact, a number of studies performed over a period spanning more than half a century—*many of which were performed by homosexuals or their sympathizers*—have shown that an extremely large percentage of sexually active homosexuals also participate in child sexual molestation.

This is not "homophobia" or "hatred," this is simple scientific fact.

For example;

- Homosexual Alfred Kinsey, the pre-eminent sexual researcher in the history of sexual research, found in 1948 that 37 percent of all male homosexuals admitted to having sex with children under 17 years old.

- A very recent (2000) study published in the *Archives of Sexual Behavior* found that "The best epidemiological evidence indicates that only 2–4% of men attracted to adults prefer men. In contrast, around 25–40% of men attracted to children prefer boys. Thus, the rate of homosexual attraction is 6–20 times higher among pedophiles."

- Another 2000 study in the *Archives of Sexual Behavior* found that ". . . all but 9 of the 48 homosexual men preferred the youngest two male age categories" for sexual activity." These age categories were fifteen and twenty years old.

- Yet another recent study in the *Archives of Sexual Behavior* found that "Pedophilia appears to have a greater than chance association with two other statistically infrequent phenomena. The first of these is homosexuality. . . . Recent surveys estimate the prevalence of homosexuality, among men attracted to adults, in the neighborhood of 2%. In contrast, the prevalence of homosexuality among pedophiles may be as high as 30–40%."

- A 1989 study in the *Journal of Sex Research* noted that ". . . the proportion of sex offenders against male children among homosexual men is substantially larger than the proportion of sex offenders against female children among heterosexual men . . . the development of pedophilia is more closely linked with homosexuality than with heterosexuality."

- A 1988 study of 229 convicted child molesters published in the *Archives of Sexual Behavior* found that 86% of pedophiles described themselves as homosexual or bisexual.

- In a 1984 *Journal of Sex and Marital Therapy* article, sex researchers found that "The proportional prevalence of [male] offenders against male children in this group of 457 offenders against children was 36 percent."

- Homosexual activists Karla Jay and Allen Young revealed in their 1979 *Gay Report* that 23% of all homosexuals have acted as "chicken hawks"—that is, they have preyed on adolescent or younger boys.

- In a 1992 study published in the *Journal of Sex and Marital Therapy*, sex researchers K. Freud and R. I. Watson found that homosexual males are three times more likely than straight men to engage in pedophilia, and that the average pedophile victimizes between 20 and 150 boys before being arrested.

- A study by sex researchers Alan Bell and Martin Weinberg found that 25% of white homosexual men have had sex with boys sixteen years and younger.

Flawed Studies

There are occasional scientific attempts to deny or obscure the fact that a disproportionately high percentage of active homosexuals also molest children. These studies are invariably afflicted with one or more fatal flaws.

A typical example, oft-quoted by gay rights activists, is the July 1994 *Pediatrics* article by [C.] Jenny, [T.A.] Roesler, and [K.L.] Poyer that finds that "Using the data from our study, the 95% confidence limits of the risk children would identify recognizably homosexual adults as the potential abuser, are from 0% to 3.1%. These limits are within current estimates of the prevalence of homosexuality in the general community."

The fatal flaw of this study is that it studied sexually abused children with a mean age of just 6.1 years. Children of this young age are usually targets of true pedophiles, those persons with no sexual attraction to adults of either sex. By contrast, homosexual pedophiles are usually classified as "ephebophiles," persons sexually attracted to pubescent or post-pubescent underage children. . . .

Definitions

The John Jay study on the sex abuse crisis in the Catholic Church in the United States defines "pedophiles" as people who "exhibit recurrent, intense, sexually arousing fantasies,

Alleged Victims of Sexual Abuse Incidents, Grouped by Gender and Age

Gender	1–7 years	8–10 years	11–14 years	15–17 years
Male	203	992	4,282	2,892
	41.7%	71.4%	85.4%	85.2%
Female	284	398	734	502
	58.3%	28.6%	14.6%	14.8%
Total per group	487	1,390	5,016	3.394
% of all incidents	5.8%	16%	50.9%	27.3%

TAKEN FROM: John Jay College of Criminal Justice, "The Nature and Scope of the Problem of Sexual Abuse of Minors by Catholic Priests and Deacons in the United States." *United States Council of Catholic Bishops, www.usccb.org.*

urges or behaviors related to sexual contact with a prepubescent child over a period of at least six months duration."

When people speak of the current crisis being a problem involving "pedophile priests," they are addressing only a small portion of the situation. According to the John Jay study, most of the sexually offending priests are not true pedophiles. They are, instead, "ephebophiles," who "exhibit these same fantasies, urges or behaviors towards post-pubescent youths." Generally, the John Jay study recognized that pedophilia can be defined as the molestation of children aged ten and younger. The National Review Board study defines "ephebophilia" as "homosexual attraction to adolescent males," a definition that certainly is validated by quotes by "gay rights" activists. . . .

Supporting Quotes by Active Homosexuals

Many homosexual leaders have openly admitted that there is a natural link between a homosexual orientation and child sexual abuse.

Many homosexual organizations and leaders not only admit to, but *support*, the sexual abuse of children by homosexuals.

An editorial in the San Francisco *Sentinel*, a member of the National Lesbian & Gay Journalist's Association, claimed that

> The love between men and boys is at the foundation of homosexuality. For the gay community to imply that boy-love is not homosexual love is ridiculous. We must not be seduced into believing misinformation from the press and the government. Child molesting does occur, but there are also positive sexual relations. And we need to support the men and the boys in those relationships.

The notorious North American Man-Boy Love Association (NAMBLA), one of several organized pedophile groups, almost always has a photo of a pre-teen boy on the cover of its *NAMBLA Bulletin*, as well as many others in its pages.

Pedophile Philip Hutchinson's poem entitled "Choirboy" is entirely typical of the fare found in the *Bulletin*;

> "You look like a cherub, but you're worldly-wise. You'd love to have me think you're newly-born, but I can spot the twinkle in your eyes; you know damned well how much you turn me on. Between us, you're the satyr—I'm the saint, so shed your sacred robe and bare your skin, surrender to my touch without restraint, and later, put your halo on again."

One of NAMBLA's flyers says that

> There is no age at which a person becomes capable of consenting to sex. The age of sexual consent is just one of many ways in which adults impose their system of control on children ... Amazing as it may seem in this child-hating and homophobic society, boy lovers [pederasts] find boys attractive and like their spontaneity and openness.

Convicted pedophile and NAMBLA member David Thorstad has said that "I think that pederasty should be given the stamp of approval. I think it's true that boy-lovers [pederasts] are much better for children than the parents are...."

Interestingly, while the mainstream press and liberal groups systematically pillory the Catholic Church, they entirely ignore the well-organized efforts by professional associations to decriminalize and normalize child sexual abuse. There exists a determined effort to decriminalize and destigmatize sexual relationships between adults and children in preparation for "normalizing" them.

For example, the American Psychiatric Association (APA) recently sponsored a symposium in which participants discussed the removal of pedophilia from an upcoming edition of the group's psychiatric manual of mental disorders. At about the same time, the *Archives of Sexual Behavior* published a special edition in December 2002 discussing whether pedophilia should remain a mental disorder.

As early as 1988, a leading American psychological journal, *Behavior Today*, claimed, "Pedophilia may be a sexual orientation rather than a sexual deviation. This raises the question as to whether pedophiles may have rights." ...

Confession of a Monsignor

It is clear, even without reference to the numerous reports throughout the recent years, that homosexuals have infiltrated the ranks of the clergy to an astonishing degree. In some corners of the Church, such behavior has long been seen as acceptable. To cite just one recent example, Msgr. Richard Sniezyk, appointed to head the Diocese of Springfield-in-Massachusetts after its bishop resigned amid sexual abuse allegations, said in an interview that the recent scandal in the Catholic Church stems from a belief among some priests during the 1960s, '70s, and '80s that sex with young men was "acceptable":

Monsignor Richard S. Sniezyk, 66, the leader of the Spring-field Diocese until the Vatican names a bishop to replace Thomas L. Dupre, said that as a seminarian and then a young priest . . . he heard of priests who had sex with young men, but "no one thought much about it" because priests didn't recognize how mentally and emotionally damaging their behavior was. . . . "It was that era of the '60s—most of it took place from the mid-'60s to the early-'80s—and the whole atmosphere out there was, it was OK, it was OK to do."

This is not a statement by an anti-Catholic partisan or some homosexual activist, but rather an admission from none other than the duly-appointed shepherd of souls in this Massachusetts diocese.

It is easy to look back on the crisis in the Catholic Church in the United States and place blame on the Vatican, on the bishops, on the seminaries, or even on our society's permissive attitude toward sexuality in general. But much terrible damage has already been done—to the victims, to the Church, and to the souls of many whose faith has been shaken or even destroyed by the scandal.

Our primary responsibilities at this point are not blame and condemnation, but reparation and prevention. We must compensate the victims, and we must reassure them by making certain that there are as few victims as possible in the future.

We often hear from the homosexual-rights movement that "gays" are "born that way." This may or may not be true, depending on which of the hundreds of conflicting studies we choose to believe.

Recognizing Weaknesses

In the most fundamental sense, this point is irrelevant. We are *all* born with weaknesses, a direct result of our fallen natures. We can deal with these weaknesses in one of two ways. We can accept them as crosses given to us by God, and we can glorify his Name by struggling to overcome them with the aid of his grace. Or we can simply give in and use the "born that way" excuse, the weak and cowardly road that is a vote of no-confidence in God's grace and its ability to save us.

Alcoholism has been proven to be genetic. Yet our spouses do not accept the "born that way" excuse if we arrive home stinking drunk every night. Kleptomania may indeed also be genetic, yet no court in the land has ever accepted the "born that way" excuse as a defense against shoplifting charges.

Alcoholics and 'kleptos' can become good and holy priests—just so long as they recognize their weaknesses, avoid near occasions of sin, and fight to overcome them on a daily basis with the help of God's grace. Men who are sexually attracted to women or other men can also become saintly priests—but *only* if they do not give in and act out their desires.

A man who is living an active homosexual lifestyle should never be ordained a priest. A man with homosexual tendencies who lives a scrupulously chaste life could be ordained a priest, and he could be a very good one, but only if he clearly recognizes the dangers and heartbreak his desires could cause in the future if he yields to them.

Recommendation

Pope John Paul II himself has set an example for dealing with our current crisis in the recent requirement he imposed upon an archbishop in Scotland. To restore the confidence of the faithful, His Holiness required a Profession of Faith be taken by Cardinal Designate Keith Patrick O'Brien on Tuesday, October 7th, 2003 at St. Mary's Cathedral, Edinburgh.

This profession of faith included the key words:

> I further state that I accept and intend to defend the law on ecclesiastical celibacy as it is proposed by the Magisterium

of the Catholic Church; I accept and promise to defend the ecclesiastical teaching about the immorality of the homosexual act; I accept and promise to promulgate always and everywhere what the Church's Magisterium teaches on contraception. So help me God and these Holy Scriptures, which I touch with my hand.

In response to the crisis of confidence in the United States generated by a gradual infiltration of homosexuals into the ranks of the clergy over the years, we propose that all clergy, regardless of rank, status, or position, be required to sign the same Profession of Faith clearly condemning all homosexual acts and precluding the clergy from advocating or approving homosexual acts, contraception, and related sins of grave immorality. We further propose that those who refuse to sign have their faculties suspended, effective immediately upon their statement of intent not to take the oath.

> *"Indeed, research supports that a child molester isn't any more likely to be homosexual than heterosexual. In fact, some research shows that for pedophiles, the gender of the child is immaterial."*

Homosexual Men Are Not More Likely than Heterosexual Men to Sexually Abuse Boys

Joe Kort

In the following viewpoint, Joe Kort addresses the issue of adult men who aren't necessarily homosexual but sexually abuse boys. Kort contends that for pedophiles the gender of the child is irrelevant, therefore neither homosexuality nor heterosexuality apply. Joe Kort, LMSW, is a psychotherapist and author of the blog Gay's Anatomy *on psychologytoday.com, as well as books on gay male development and gay male couples. He is a gay and lesbian studies adjunct professor at Wayne State University.*

As you read, consider the following questions:

1. According to the author, what are two reasons gender is immaterial to a pedophile?

Joe Kort, "Homosexuality and Pedophilia: The False Link," *Psychology Today,* September 15, 2008. Copyright © 1991-2008 Sussex Publishers LLC. Reproduced by permission.

2. The author cites research psychologist Gregory Herek. Why does Herek believe most people in today's society immediately think of male-male molestation as homosexuality?

3. Why does the author agree female-female molestation is "unthinkable"?

When discussing sexual abuse and molestation of children, there's often conflict over terminology. One frequently quoted researcher on the topic of homosexuality and child molestation, Gregory Herek, a research psychologist at the University of California, defines pedophilia as "a psychosexual disorder characterized by a preference for prepubescent children as sexual partners, which may or may not be acted upon." He defines child sexual abuse as "actual sexual contact between an adult and someone who has not reached the legal age of consent." Not all pedophiles actually molest children, he points out. A pedophile may be attracted to children, but never actually engage in sexual contact with them. Quite often, pedophiles never develop a sexual orientation toward other adults.

Pedophiles are Aroused by Youth, Not Gender

Herek points out that child molestation and child sexual abuse refer to "actions," without implying any "particular psychological makeup or motive on the part of the perpetrator." In other words, not all incidents of child sexual abuse are perpetrated by pedophiles. Pedophilia can be viewed as a kind of sexual fetish, wherein the person requires the mental image of a child—not necessarily a flesh-and-blood child—to achieve sexual gratification. Rarely does a pedophile experience sexual desire for adults of either gender. They usually don't identify as homosexual. The majority identify as heterosexual, even those who abuse children of the same gender. They are sexually aroused by youth, not by gender. In contrast, child molesters often exert power and control over children in an effort to dominate them. They do experience sexual desire for adults, but molest children episodically, for reasons apart from sexual desire, much as rapists enjoy power, violence and controlling their humiliated victims. Indeed, research supports that a child molester isn't any more likely to be homosexual than heterosexual.

In fact, some research shows that for pedophiles, the gender of the child is immaterial. Accessibility is more the factor in who a pedophile abuses. This may explain the high incidence of children molested in church communities and fraternal organizations, where the pedophile may more easily have access to children. In these situations, an adult male is trusted by those around him, including children and their families. Males are often given access to boys to mentor, teach, coach and advise. Therefore, a male pedophile may have easier access to a male child. In trying to make sense of an adult male's sexually abusing a male child, many of us mislabel it as an act of homosexuality, which it isn't.

Feminists have argued for years that rape is not a sex act, it is an act of violence using sex as a weapon. In the same way, a pedophile abusing a child of the same sex is not perpetrating a homosexual act, but an act of violence and exploitation using sexuality. There is a world of difference between these two things, but it requires a subtle understanding of the inner motivation of the abuser.

Homosexuality Does Not Apply

To call child molestation of a boy by a man "homosexual" or of a girl by a man "heterosexual" is to misunderstand pedophilia. No true pedophile is attracted to adults, so neither homosexuality nor heterosexuality applies. Accordingly, Herek suggests calling men's sexual abuse of boys "male-male molestation" and men's abuse of girls, "male-female molestation."

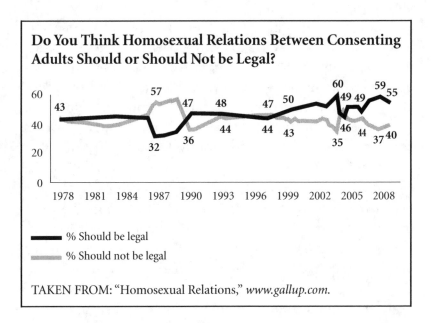

Do You Think Homosexual Relations Between Consenting Adults Should or Should Not be Legal?

■ % Should be legal

░ % Should not be legal

TAKEN FROM: "Homosexual Relations," *www.gallup.com.*

Interestingly, Anna C. Salter writes, in "Predators, Pedophiles, Rapists and other Sex Offenders," that when a man molests little girls, we call him a "pedophile" and not a "heterosexual." Of course, when a man molests little boys, people say outright, or mutter under their breath, "homosexual." Herek writes that because of our society's aversion to male homosexuality, and the attempts made by some to represent gay men as a danger to "family values," many in our society immediately think of male-male molestation as homosexuality. He compares this with the time when African Americans were often falsely accused of raping white women, and when medieval Jews were accused of murdering Christian babies in ritual sacrifices. Both are examples of how mainstream society eagerly jumped to conclusions that justified discrimination and violence against these minorities. Today, gays face the same kind of prejudice. Most recently, we've seen gay men unfairly turned out of the Boy Scouts of America on the basis of this myth that gay men are likely to be child molesters. Keeping gays out of scouting won't protect boys from pedophiles.

In reality, abuse of boys by gay pedophiles is rare, and the abuse of girls by lesbians is rarer still. Nicholas Groth is a noted authority on this topic. In a 1982 study by Grot, he asks, "Are homosexual adults in general sexually attracted to children, and are pre-adolescent children at greater risk of molestation from homosexual adults than from heterosexual adults? There is no reason to believe so. The research to date all points to there being no significant relationship between a homosexual lifestyle and child molestation. There appears to be practically no reportage of sexual molestation of girls by lesbian adults, and the adult male who sexually molests young boys is not likely to be homosexual." Herek writes, similarly, that abuse of boys by gay men is rare; and that the abuse of girls by lesbians is rarer still.

Female-Female Molestation

The topic of female-female molestation continues to be largely ignored. There are few books on female sex offenders, particularly about mothers sexually abusing their daughters. I can find only one book on mothers who sexually abuse their sons by Hani Miletski, M.S.W., entitled, *Mother-Son Incest: The Unthinkable Taboo*. Unthinkable is an appropriate word—so much so that there is nothing else in the literature on this topic, even though female pedophiles and female child molesters certainly exist.

We know so much more than we did historically and yet have a long way to go. We can understand child sexual abuse further when people's bias and prejudice are removed and the evidence is empirical and scientific.

Periodical Bibliography

The following articles have been selected to supplement the diverse views presented in this chapter.

Associated Press	"Children at Higher Risk in Nontraditional Homes: Abusive-boyfriend Syndrome Part of the Broader Trend, Experts Worry," November 18, 2007.
Diana Buchanan	"Child Abuse and Neglect in the Military: An Introduction for Child Welfare Lawyers," *Child Law Practice Newsletter*, vol. 26, no. 10, December 2007, pp. 145–49.
Deborah Gibbs, Sandra Martin, Ruby Johnson, E. Rentz, Monique Clinton-Sherrod, and Jennifer Hardison	"Child Maltreatment and Substance Abuse Among U.S. Army Soldiers," *Child Maltreatment*, vol. 13, no. 3, 2008, pp. 259–268.
Frank Greeve	"Fear of Internet Predators Unfounded, Study Finds," *McClatchy Newspapers*, February 18, 2008. www.mcclatchydc.com/homepage/story/28029.html.
Darla Hernandez	"Special Report: Brutal Boyfriends and Child Abuse," February 8, 2007. www.wsbt.com/news/local/5586701.html.
T.K. Kenyon	"Internet Sexual Predators: The New War is Words," *Suite101.com*, February 15, 2007. http://sexual-abuse.suite101.com/article.cfm/internet_sexual_predators.
Public Broadcasting System (PBS)	"Growing Up Online," *Frontline*, January 22, 2008. www.pbs.org/wgbh/pages/frontline/kidsonline/view/main.html.
Kevonne Small and Janine M. Zweig	"Sexual Victimization of Youth," *The Prevention Researcher*, vol. 14, no. 2, April 2007, pp. 3–5.

OPPOSING
VIEWPOINTS®
SERIES

CHAPTER 3

How Does Child Abuse Affect Its Victims?

Chapter Preface

In a *New York Times Magazine* article, writer Emily Bazelon tells the story of two sisters, La'Tanya and Tichelle. For at least five years, both sisters were repeatedly sexually molested by their mother's live-in boyfriend. Although their mother warned him to stay away from her daughters and even installed a lock on the girls' bedroom door, in the end, she failed to protect them. Eventually social services became involved, the girls were removed from the home for a time, and the boyfriend was arrested, convicted, and sentenced to eighty-five years in prison.

Despite their childhood trauma, the sisters graduated from high school and obtained decent jobs, their own apartments, and their own cars. For the poor neighborhood in which they grew up, they have beaten the odds. For the younger sister, Tichelle, the journey has been less difficult. She enjoyed high school, forgave her mother, and easily began a career. The abuse however, has had a more lasting effect on La'Tanya. Even in high school the world seemed burdensome for her. At fifteen years old and still angry at her mother, La'Tanya moved in with her seventeen-year-old boyfriend and—wanting to be loved—had a baby. She has struggled with recurring nightmares about the abuse, with panic attacks that send her to the emergency room, and with day-long crying spells.

What accounts for Tichelle's greater capacity for resilience? Why do some people, but not others, bounce back from childhood abuse? Of course, no two cases are the same. Even in this case of two sisters abused by the same man, La'Tanya *did* have a heavier burden. She was abused for more years than Tichelle, and as the oldest sister in a dysfunctional household, she practically raised her sister.

For many decades, scientists have looked for the answer to why a minority of abused children *do* exceed expectations. Research has shown that having a positive relationship with trustworthy adults is one of the most reliable predictors of an abuse survivor's ability to overcome adversity, and having high intelligence is another predictor. In this case both sisters probably beat the odds because they did have a great deal of support from adults, including a positive relationship with the *New York Times* writer.

In the past few years, however, researchers have identified one genetic component to resiliency that may also, at least partially, explain why Tichelle has been better able than La'Tanya to bounce back from trauma. The particular gene in question, called 5-HTT, regulates serotonin, a chemical that transmits signals between the nerve cells and the brain. The proper regulation of serotonin in the brain protects people from the effects of stress and trauma, particularly depression.

Everyone's 5-HTT gene has two components, or alleles. Each allele can be one of two versions: long or short. The more long alleles a person has the better their serotonin is regulated and the more likely he or she is to overcome adversity, according to researchers. One study found that childhood abuse was a predictor for depression in adulthood, but only in subjects with at least one short allele. Meanwhile, subjects who had experienced severe abuse in childhood and who had two short alleles were found to have a 63 percent risk for major depression.

Controlled experiments with animals have reinforced the theory that genetics is a powerful factor in predicting resilience after poor parenting. In one study, monkeys who were raised by their peers and not their mothers and who had one short 5-HTT allele, and therefore lower levels of serotonin, consistently reacted aggressively and fearfully to monkeys who were strangers. Meanwhile, monkeys who were also raised by their peers and not their mothers, but had two long alleles tended not to panic, but reacted more like the monkeys raised by mothers.

Scientists and other experts stress that genes alone do not determine resiliency one way or the other. This particular gene in no way causes depression and in fact seems only to be triggered in such dire circumstances as abuse, including severe neglect. As with the monkeys, a loving adult is as important to a child—especially to an abused child—as is the child's genetic make up in predicting his or her ability to thrive in adulthood.

How circumstances and genes help children and adults cope with the effects of child abuse is worthy of further research and discussion. The viewpoints in this chapter discuss the damaging effects of child abuse and the coping strategies that can help children rise above these effects.

> "*Researchers are discovering how early experiences affect the ability to maintain psychological and physical balance. Childhood trauma and loss can cause prolonged hypersensitivity to stress by upsetting the regulation of the HPA axis and sympathetic nervous system.*"

Abuse May Disrupt Brain Development in Children

Harvard Mental Health Letter

If young children are abused or suffer constant stress, changes can occur in the brain that may cause psychiatric disorders even into adulthood. This viewpoint explains the biology behind these changes, some of the disorders that can result, and some potential methods for reversing the damage. The Harvard Mental Health Letter *is a newsletter for laymen and professionals published by Harvard Medical School.*

As you read, consider the following questions:

1. If the hypothalamic-pituitary-adrenal axis and sympathetic nervous system are activated by stress, what physical and mental responses occur?

2. What happens when the stress response, as described above, activates too frequently?

3. In an experiment, what helped anxious rat pups respond much better to stress as adults?

Scientists are discovering that early experiences can have profound long-term effects on the biological systems that govern responses to stress. If these systems lack the environment required for normal development, they may fail to function as evolution designed them. Effects on the maturing brain can be subtle as well as obvious. Disturbances at a critical time early in life may exert a disproportionate influence, creating the conditions for childhood and adult depression, anxiety, and post-traumatic stress symptoms.

The Biology

The body and brain adapt to acute stress—originally, a threat to survival or bodily integrity—through the activity of the hypothalamic-pituitary-adrenal (HPA) axis and the sympathetic nervous system. The hypothalamus, at the base of the brain, secretes corticotropin-releasing factor (CRF), which stimulates the pituitary gland to release adrenocorticotropic hormone (ACTH). ACTH travels to the adrenal glands and causes the release of the stress hormones cortisol and adrenaline (epinephrine), mobilizing the body and mind for fighting or fleeing. Blood pressure and blood sugar levels rise, breathing and heart rate increase, muscles tense, and we feel anger, anxiety, or fear. The system is controlled by feedback: A high level of stress hormones signals the hypothalamus to stop issuing CRF. Along with the HPA axis, the sympathetic nervous system is activated, as CRF influences circuits that use the neurotransmitters dopamine, norepinephrine, and serotonin.

If the stress response is provoked too often or for too long, it becomes less adaptive. A person under chronic stress, with no hope of relief, is constantly on guard and never able to relax, psychologically or physiologically. The feedback mechanism loses its sensitivity, and the system fails to shut off.

Stress and Depression

Depression bears some resemblance to an acute stress response that persists when it is no longer needed. The adrenal glands produce more cortisol, and an injection of the synthetic stress hormone dexamethasone often does not have the normal feedback effect of suppressing the release of cortisol. Depressed persons may have excess CRF in the spinal fluid and greater expression (activation) of genes for producing CRF receptors in the brain, especially the centers of memory and strong emotions in the hippocampus and amygdala. Instead of being temporarily and appropriately alert and vigilant, a depressed person is likely to be either chronically lethargic and apathetic or agitated, anxious, and sleepless.

Maltreatment and Psychiatric Disorders

It has long been known that childhood abuse and neglect and the loss of a parent are associated with adult psychiatric disorders, including depression, anxiety, and post-traumatic symptoms. Apart from heredity and recent stress, child maltreatment is the most common predictor of major depression in adults. Now researchers are discovering how early experiences affect the ability to maintain psychological and physical balance. Childhood trauma and loss can cause prolonged hypersensitivity to stress by upsetting the regulation of the HPA axis and sympathetic nervous system.

Receptors in the brain are sensitive to CRF in infancy and even before birth. A depressed mother raises the level of CRF in the child she is carrying. Six-month-old children of women who were depressed or abused while pregnant secrete cortisol at a higher than average level in response to mild stress.

Some of these effects can be demonstrated experimentally in laboratory animals. Rat pups were removed from their

Post-traumatic Stress Disorder: Risk Factors

	Event	Individual	Family and Social
Increase Risk *(Prolong the intensity or duration of the acute stress response)*	• Multiple or repeated event (e.g., domestic violence or physical abuse) • Physical injury to child • Involves physical injury or death to loved one, particularly mother • Dismembered or disfigured bodies seen • Destroys home, school or community • Disrupts community infrastructure (e.g., earthquake) • Perpetrator is family member • Long duration (e.g., flood)	• Female • Age (Younger more vulnerable) • Subjective perception of physical harm • History of previous exposure to trauma • No cultural or religious anchors • No shared experience with peers (experiential isolation) • Low IQ • Pre-existing neuropsychiatric disorder (especially anxiety related)	• Trauma directly impacts caregivers • Anxiety in primary caregivers • Continuing threat and disruption to family • Chaotic, overwhelmed family • Physical isolation • Distant caregiving • Absent caregivers
Decrease Risk *(Decrease intensity or duration of the acute stress response)*	• Single event • Perpetrator is stranger • No disruption of family or community structure • Short duration (e.g., tornado)	• Cognitively capable of understanding abstract concepts • Healthy coping skills • Educated about normative post-traumatic responses • Immediate post-traumatic interventions	• Intact, nurturing family supports • Non-traumatized caregivers • Caregivers educated about normative post-traumatic responses • Strong family beliefs

TAKEN FROM: http://www.childtrauma.org.

mothers repeatedly before weaning. The mothers tended to neglect pups treated this way, giving them little attention and feeding them last. When tested as adults, the rats overreacted to mild stress and were more likely to suffer from a rat equivalent of depression—passivity in difficult situations and a weak response to rewards like sugar water. Young hamsters placed in a cage with mature hamsters that threaten and attack them show lasting changes in the brain circuitry using serotonin and other neurotransmitters that regulate mood and aggression.

Maltreatment and Post Traumatic Stress Disorder

People who suffer childhood maltreatment are more vulnerable to post-traumatic stress symptoms after further traumatic childhood or adult experiences because their bodies and brains have "learned" that they cannot count on protection and solace in distressing situations. The symptoms of post-traumatic stress disorder (PTSD) include heightened anxiety and jumpiness, intrusive memories and flashbacks, avoidance of situations, places, and people reminiscent of the traumatic event, and often emotional numbness, loss of trust in others, and an aversion to intimate relationships.

PTSD is usually preceded by an acute stress reaction that involves activity of the HPA axis and sympathetic nervous system. The amygdala, the brain's center for registering fear, intensifies memories of trauma through its links to the hypothalamus, hippocampus, and cerebral cortex. The aroused amygdala strengthens connections that produce emotionally charged memories. Its function is to make these memories difficult to eradicate so that we will recognize the threat if it reappears. In this way, traumatic experiences are preserved in long-term memory, and anything even remotely reminiscent of the trauma may serve as a cue to revive the experience. Re-experiencing further strengthens the emotional associations, which in turn further consolidates the memory in a vicious cycle.

PTSD Changes the Brain

Excess cortisol production can damage the hippocampus, disrupting the connections between neurons and eventually cause the neurons themselves to degenerate. Brain-derived neurotrophic factor (BDNF), which helps the hippocampus to generate neurons, is reduced in rats who have been separated from their mothers. One study found a shrunken hippocampus in depressed women who were traumatized as children. In another study, women with post-traumatic stress disorder resulting from child abuse showed abnormal activity in the frontal lobes.

Reversing PTSD

Researchers are looking for ways to prevent and reverse the harm, either in childhood or later in life. Rat pups from a genetically anxious strain respond much better to stress as adults if they are adopted by unusually attentive foster mothers who constantly lick and groom them. In a strain of rats sensitive to alcohol, the risk of addiction is increased by early separation from their mothers. Selective serotonin reuptake inhibitors (Prozac and company) may partially reverse the effect. These drugs may also promote the regeneration of neurons in the hippocampus.

Drugs that interfere with the activity of CRF are being considered for the treatment of depression. Mifepristone (RU-486), best known as an abortion drug, is a CRF antagonist that has shown some promise as a treatment for psychotic depression. Propranolol (Inderal), a drug that blocks nerve receptors for norepinephrine in the amygdala, apparently reduces arousal in response to memories of a traumatic experience when it is taken for several weeks starting immediately after the trauma. It could be warding off PTSD by preventing traumatic memories from working their way indelibly into the brain.

Psychological treatment for post-traumatic stress disorder also involves retraining the amygdala to respond differently when traumatic memories recur. And it may turn out that sometimes the nature of the childhood experience determines the choice of treatment. In one study, an antidepressant was compared to cognitive behavioral therapy and a combination of the two in the treatment of severely depressed women. The combination was best for the group as a whole, but for those who had suffered traumatic experiences in childhood, the drug was less effective than psychotherapy and the combination was no better than psychotherapy alone.

Each Case Is Different

Maltreatment does not, of course, cause the same changes in neurotransmitter or stress hormone activity or long-term brain function in everyone. Individual genetic characteristics are important; for example, there is evidence that one variant of a gene that governs the reabsorption of serotonin promotes greater activity in the amygdala and makes children more vulnerable to stress. The kind of stress—parental loss; neglect; physical, sexual, or emotional abuse—may also make a difference. And some maltreated children, instead of developing adult psychiatric disorders, come through relatively unscathed.

Learning more about the biological consequences of child maltreatment through brain imaging and molecular genetic studies will help in defining more precisely the causes and nature of depression, anxiety, and post-traumatic stress symptoms. Just as important, it may improve our understanding of how resilient children maintain hope, control anxiety, and achieve normal development despite abuse and neglect.

| *"Children with trauma were being misdiagnosed as having attention-deficit/ hyperactivity disorder."*

Children Exposed to Domestic Violence Suffer Emotional and Behavioral Problems

Avril Roberts

Many children are not physically abused, yet they witness physical abuse in their homes. According to this viewpoint new attention is being given to such children. For example, some shelters for abused women have developed programs to help children manage the impact of abuse. In addition, the author discusses recent efforts to coordinate agency responses to provide better services for these children as well as initiatives to change laws to recognize witness to abuse as abuse itself. Avril Roberts writes for CrossCurrents, *a publication of the Centre for Addiction and Mental Health.*

As you read, consider the following questions:

1. Children who witness domestic violence have been found to exhibit what behaviors?

Avril Roberts, "Home is Where the Hurt Is: Children Exposed to Domestic Violence Face Psychological Woes," *CrossCurrents*, Summer 2007, pp. 12–13. Copyright © 2007 Centre for Addiction and Mental Health. Reproduced by permission.

2. What are the many merits of coordinated services?

3. In Ontario, Canada, after authorities changed the laws to include living with domestic violence as a form of domestic violence, how much did the number of reported cases increase?

A group of pre-schoolers enters a playroom scattered with toys. One child heads straight for the police car, picks it up and runs it along the floor, announcing, "The police car is coming to the house to stop the daddy from hitting the mommy."

This scenario illustrates young children's acute awareness of violence in the home. But while the effects of child abuse are well documented, how about children exposed to domestic violence? With Statistics Canada estimating that between 1999 and 2004 258,000 Canadian children were exposed to an assault on their mother, it's an issue that can't be ignored.

Witnessing Abuse

"These children can suffer the same aftermath in terms of emotional and behavioural problems as being abused directly," says Dr. Peter Jaffe, academic director at the Centre for Research on Violence Against Women and Children at the University of Western Ontario in London. They may exhibit anxiety, depression, agitation, aggression, defiance or learning difficulties. Research also shows that children exposed to domestic violence are themselves at risk for abuse and for becoming a perpetrator or victim later in life.

Jaffe says it's not just what children actually witness that is harmful: "The term 'exposure' takes into account the variety of ways in which children may be exposed to domestic violence," he says. "What they see, what they hear from their bedroom at night, what they experience in the aftermath of violence when they walk into the kitchen after school."

Programs Help

B.C. [British Columbia] is leading the way in helping these children with its integrated Children Who Witness Abuse (CWWA) programs created and coordinated by the B.C./ Yukon Society of Transition Houses (BCYSTH). Launched in 1993 out of the realization that the needs of children who were coming into transition shelters with their abused mothers weren't being addressed, the programs offer support and information for mothers, and group and individual counselling for children and youth aged 3–18. The programs promote healing by helping children with the emotional, behavioural and social impact of exposure to their mothers' abuse. Groups are organized by age or specific experience and run from 10 to 12 weeks.

"Through groups, children break their isolation. They hear other children's experiences and offer support to each other in their own ways," says Shahnaz Rahman, co-ordinator of Children's Services for the BCYSTH. While the CWWA program emphasizes group support, individual counselling is provided when a child's trauma is severe or if a child is not ready to participate in a group. Topics like safety planning are discussed and very young children learn how to call 911. Specific concerns are also addressed in group and individual counseling: In her former position as a CWWA counsellor, Rahman conducted sessions on grief and loss, separation and boundaries, when she facilitated a group where separation from the dad was a pressing issue.

Role Models

To counteract the negative role modeling of abusive fathers, the groups often have male and female co-facilitators. That's also the case at the Child Development Institute in Toronto, which offers Here to Help, an early intervention program for children exposed to woman abuse: "We do that strategically so children have an opportunity to see healthy male-female relationships and sharing of power," says Angélique Jenney, director of Family Violence Services.

Here to Help and the CWWA programs target children living in a relatively stable environment—away from the abuser. "Children's safety can be compromised if counselling is done while they are still living with the abuser," Rahman explains. "It becomes another secret for them to keep. They may also be learning new skills like assertiveness or expressing feelings, which may not be safe to do with the abuser at home." Most children in the CWWA programs live with their mothers in transition shelters, but programs also run through other community agencies that service women.

Play Therapy

Here to Help, for children aged 4–16, combines psycho-education with age-appropriate play therapy. The work with kids aged 4–6 uses puppets, art and toys. "Children's play represents their internal model of the world," says Ramona Alaggia, associate professor in the Faculty of Social Work at the University of Toronto. "Their representation of what they think is going on is expressed that way."

Jenney agrees: "It is much easier for young kids to manage their emotional involvement at that level. Through play, children can integrate difficult life experiences into internal representations and understandings of the world around them, which helps them cope and leads to positive outcomes."

Counselling

Children aged 7–9 have more verbal skills, but according to Jenney, they may have a distorted cognitive understanding of why the violence is happening. A child may accept the father's excuses without knowing the whole story. With this age group, counselling includes examining situations and exploring possibilities.

At all age levels, renewed contact with the abusing parent is a constant concern. "Most children in our program have ac-

The Effects of Domestic Violence on Children

Statistics

- Each year an estimated 3.3 million children are exposed to violence against their mothers or female caretakers by family members.

- A survey of 6,000 American families found that 50 percent of men who assault their wives also abuse their children.

- Research shows that 80 to 90 percent of children living in homes where there is domestic violence are aware of the violence.

- A number one predictor of child abuse is woman abuse.

- The more severe the abuse of the mother, the worse the child abuse.

- Some 80 percent of child fatalities within the family are attributable to fathers or father surrogates.

- In families where the mother is assaulted by the father, daughters are at risk of sexual abuse [at a rate] 6.51 times greater than girls in non-abusive families.

- A child's exposure to the father abusing the mother is the strongest risk factor for transmitting violent behavior from one generation to the next.

- Male children who witness the abuse of mothers by fathers are more likely to become men who batter in adulthood than those male children from homes free of violence.

The Alabama Coalition Against Domestic Violence,
http://www.acadv.org/.

cess to their father at some point," says Jenney. "A lot of men unfortunately use this opportunity to continue to be abusive to their partners." A common tactic is sending coded messages, promises or objects to the mother via the child.

Coordinated Services

Given the far-reaching tentacles of domestic violence—involvement with shelters, police, child protection agencies, family and criminal courts, schools—the ideal intervention and support program would occur within the context of coordinated or integrated services.

B.C.'s CWWA network provides just that sort of centrally coordinated community-based structure. The network is coordinated provincially by the BCYSTH, and individual programs are funded either solely or jointly by the B.C. Ministry of Community Services or the Ministry of Children and Family Development.

Coordinated services have many merits: They provide capacity for developing and promoting best practices and quality control; they facilitate learning and cross-training among disciplines; and they create synergies for dealing more effectively with government agencies and advocating for program funding.

A Misdiagnosis

For example, the realization that children with trauma were being misdiagnosed as having attention-deficit/hyperactivity disorder (ADHD) prompted the BCYSTH to work more closely with the B.C. Children's Hospital to improve understanding of the overlap between ADHD and post traumatic stress disorder and build partnerships between mental health workers and CWWA counsellors. A handbook for teachers has also been developed as part of the Violence Is Preventable project, which operates in 28 elementary and secondary schools in B.C. to ensure that students affected by domestic violence receive support.

Domestic violence treatment services elsewhere are not as cohesive. Ontario has 63 Early Intervention Programs for Child Witnesses of Woman Abuse. Created in 2000, the programs are funded by the Ministry of Community and Social Services but are not centrally coordinated for the province. Here to Help is offered through six community agencies in Toronto—the Child Development Institute, Jewish Family and Child Service, Le Centre medico-social communautaire, Native Child and Family Services of Toronto, Yorktown Child and Family Centre and the YWCA.

Better Child Welfare Legislation

Child welfare agencies, for their part, have made strides toward community collaboration, due partly to changes in child welfare legislation. In 2000, following several high-profile coroner's inquests into domestic violence-related deaths, Ontario strengthened the section of the Child and Family Services Act about emotional harm to a child. Living with domestic violence is now identified as a form of emotional or psychological abuse. The change saw a 400 per cent increase in reporting of domestic violence cases to Ontario's children's aid societies (CAS) between 2000 and 2003.

Meanwhile, workers in women's shelters found themselves caught between retaining the trust and confidentiality of their women clients and reporting their clients to CAS. Children's aid societies were forced to take a closer look at their practices to determine the best approaches for child protection workers dealing with domestic violence cases.

Working Together

In 2004, the Toronto CAS implemented a collaboration agreement for the Children's Aid Societies and Violence Against Women (VAW) Agencies of Toronto. "It outlines eight intersection points where we meet, where we work together and it outlines how we should be working together and the steps we should take," says Lisa Tomlinson, supervisor of the domestic violence team at the Children's Aid Society of Toronto, which handles almost 5,000 domestic violence cases a year.

Similar CAS/VAW protocols have been implemented by all children's aid societies across Ontario to enhance their relationship with agencies serving women exposed to domestic abuse, thereby improving services to children and mothers.

Ontario CAS recently introduced a differential response for all calls coming into their screening departments so they can assess immediately if a family needs a CAS investigation or if other community agencies can provide a better response. "We want to ensure everybody is safe—the woman and the child," says Tomlinson. This fall [2007], the Ontario Association of Children's Aid Societies plans to launch a Best Practices document and a new training program about domestic violence for child protection workers.

| "Society reinforces the notion that boys and young men should be able to protect themselves from harm and not talk about painful experiences."

Abuse in Childhood Impacts the Sexual, Reproductive, and Parenting Behaviors of Young Men

Patricia Paluzzi and Abby Kahn

Society seems to pay little attention to male victims of domestic violence and sexual abuse, and male victims themselves also are less likely to report it. This viewpoint explains why abuse is different for boys than it is for girls, and discusses the impact of abuse on the sexual behavior, reproductive health outcomes, and parenting behaviors of young men. Patricia Paluzzi is a mental health professional and president and CEO of Healthy Teen Network, and Abby Kahn is the program and policy associate for Healthy Teen Network.

Patricia Paluzzi and Abby Kahn, "The Impact of Child Maltreatment and Family Violence on the Sexual, Reproductive, and Parenting Behaviors of Young Men," *The Prevention Researcher*, December 2007, vol. 14, pp. 8–10. Copyright © 2007 Integrated Research Services, Inc. Reproduced by permission

As you read, consider the following questions:

1. Compared with females who witness family violence, what behaviors and conditions are increased in male children who witness family violence?

2. Approximately what percentage of abused males had not talked to anyone about their abuse, according to one national school-based survey?

3. What two theories might explain why male survivors of sexual abuse are more likely to be involved in a teen pregnancy than female survivors of sexual abuse?

We are all familiar with the phrase, "Boys will be Boys." It is often given as a tongue-in-cheek response to aggressive or "boyish" behavior; the kind of roughhousing or bullying more often tolerated—or even encouraged—among boys than girls. Such a strict and outmoded definition of masculinity serves as one major barrier to boys and young men who seek the opportunity to disclose abuse, discuss their experiences of child maltreatment and family violence, and receive treatment. This lack of disclosure masks the very real problem of abuse among males and permits all of us to continue to use the same narrow lens to view males as solely perpetrators and seldom survivors of violence. Research tells us that boys are in fact exposed to child maltreatment and family violence and this exposure can lead to higher rates of sexually transmitted infections (STIs), including HIV, involvement in a teen pregnancy, and even perpetrating violence in their own intimate relationships as well as with their children.

The problem of child maltreatment and family violence is clear—what we lack is public attention to this issue as it affects boys and young men. . . .

Scope of the Problem

Child maltreatment is a serious problem; however, the quality of national surveillance data on child maltreatment is poor.

Our best estimates of the prevalence of child maltreatment and family violence come from studies using large, national samples that cut across social groups, such as the National Longitudinal Study of Adolescent Health (Add Health). Collected between 1994 and 1995, the Add Health study reported that 41.5% of males experienced supervision neglect, 28.4% experienced physical assault, 11.8% experienced physical neglect, and 4.5% experienced sexual abuse involving physical contact.

The Male Experience of Child Maltreatment and Family Violence

The male experience of child maltreatment and family violence is unique from that of female survivors in several significant ways. The gendered socialization that males undergo affects the types of maltreatment males are exposed to, the psychological effects, and the resulting behavioral sequelae [consequence]. Worldwide, males are more often the victims of beatings and physical punishment and in the U.S. are more often forced to participate in non-penetrative sex acts.

The gender of the perpetrator has also been shown to significantly influence how a male child is affected in cases of witnessing family violence. When a father perpetrates physical and/or psychological abuse against a mother, male child witnesses show a greater tendency to develop certain conditions, such as internalizing behaviors (depression, disordered eating, etc.), externalizing behaviors (binge drinking, fighting, etc.), and post-traumatic stress disorder than female witnesses.

Possibly the most troubling aspect of the male experience of child maltreatment and family violence is that male survivors tend to report their victimization less frequently. According to one national, school-based survey, nearly half (48%) of abused males had not talked to anyone about their abuse. One reason that male survivors report their victimization less often is that society reinforces the notion that boys and young men should be able to protect themselves from harm and not talk about painful experiences. Thus, male survivors may interpret their experiences of maltreatment as a failure to protect themselves and reporting it as a public admission of this failure. Male survivors may also fear loss of their independence or other negative repercussions from disclosing their abuse. Male survivors may fear that if law enforcement or Child Protective Services intervenes and they are removed from their home and placed in a facility or in foster care, then they somehow failed to "be a man" and manage their problems independently.

Males may not report their experiences of sexual abuse in particular because in many places in the world, such victimization holds the social stigma of being associated with homosexual behavior. In a society that does not wholly accept homosexuality, fear of being gay or perceived as being gay can add to the psychological trauma of sexual victimization for a male survivor. Such limited and strict social and cultural expectations on men place unique challenges on male survivors in every aspect of their experience from self-disclosure and disclosure to others, through treatment and recovery.

The Impact on Sexual Behavior

Among male survivors, sexual initiation at a young age, whether recognized as abuse or not, has been shown to increase the risk of subsequent adverse and/or health compromising sexual and reproductive outcomes, as well as abusive behaviors within intimate or family relationships. Male survivors of child sexual abuse are more likely to engage in sex with more lifetime partners, as well as engage in prostitution, often after running away from home and/or to support a habit of substance use. Early initiation of sexual activity whether consensual or coerced can lead to casual sex with multiple sexual partners, with those males who were youngest at the time of first sex reporting the most lifetime sexual part-

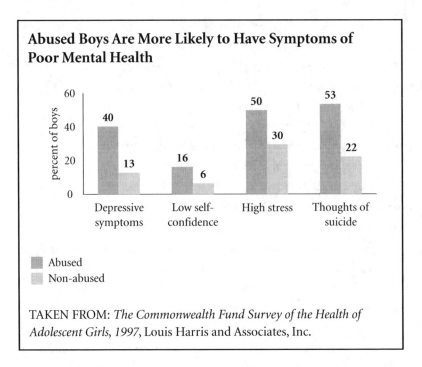

Abused Boys Are More Likely to Have Symptoms of Poor Mental Health

TAKEN FROM: *The Commonwealth Fund Survey of the Health of Adolescent Girls, 1997*, Louis Harris and Associates, Inc.

ners. Survivors of early exposure to child sexual abuse may report more liberal attitudes toward sex, the belief that it is okay to have multiple partners, and that it is not okay to say "no" to sex.

The experience of child maltreatment and family violence is a strong predictor that adolescent males will perpetrate acts of violence, including dating violence, intimate partner violence, as well as sexual violence not specific to intimate relationships in the form of rape, child molestation, and/or verbal coercion. Adolescent males with a history of sexual abuse are shown to be more than twice as likely to perpetrate sexual violence as their non-abused peers.

Reproductive Health Outcomes

Exposure to child maltreatment or family violence during childhood increases the likelihood that males will engage in behaviors that put them at greater risk than their non-abused peers for adverse reproductive health outcomes such as contracting an STI, including HIV/AIDS, and involvement in a teen pregnancy. Male survivors of sexual abuse perpetrated by a non-family member only were twice as likely to report having had an STI, and survivors of both incest and extra-familial sexual abuse were seven times as likely to report having had an STI, as their non-abused peers. Men who report early abuse have higher HIV/AIDS rates, not explained by intravenous drug use, than those with no history of victimization.

Exposure to child maltreatment, specifically sexual abuse, among males has been linked to higher rates of involvement in a teen pregnancy than among their non-abused peers. Male survivors of sexual abuse are more likely to be involved in a pregnancy than their abused female counterparts, even though females are more than four times as likely to report sexual abuse. The likelihood that a male will become involved in a teen pregnancy increases even more when two or more forms of any type of abuse are present. In a society that expects men to be dominant, producing a child can be a way to reestablish a sense of masculinity and virility that are questioned through victimization. In a society that fears homosexuality in any form, impregnating a female may alleviate some of the gender identity confusion caused by sexual abuse in which the perpetrator is also male.

Parenting Behaviors

Parents with a developmental history characterized by child maltreatment and family violence are more likely to maltreat their own children later in life. Exposure to child maltreatment or family violence as boys and young men has been linked to perpetration of family violence and the replication of abusive parenting styles and attitudes as fathers, including both emotional rejection and physical neglect of their own children. . . .

Boys will be boys—that is, as long as we, both as individuals and a society, continue to reinforce a version of male gender identity that breeds negativity and violence among boys and young men. As long as we continue to view males as solely perpetrators and seldom survivors of abuse, we will fail to prevent violence and instead add to the trauma male survivors have already been dealt. We must find a way to teach boys that, to "be a man" does not mean ascribing to outdated and harmful notions of masculinity. Paradigm shifts do occur, and they usually begin when concerned individuals take the lead in calling for action. Let each of us strive to ensure every young man has the opportunity to feel accepted and supported, to reach his potential, and to live a full, healthy, and rewarding life.

> "I feel ... disbelief that we have been running circles around the central issue of this man's life for as long as I have known him."

Unreleased Emotions from Child Abuse Can Create Devastating Anger

Jon O. Neher

In this viewpoint the author, a family physician, recounts an examination of a fifty-year-old patient who had been under the physician's care for ten years. Dr. Neher describes many of the patient's physical and emotional symptoms and the physical and emotional results of the patient's unreleased anger, all caused by long-term physical and sexual abuse the patient experienced as a child. Jon O. Neher is a family physician in Renton, Washington.

As you read, consider the following questions:

1. Why was Mr. Kelley fired from his job?
2. How did Dr. Neher know that Mr. Kelley's anger management sessions had been successful?
3. What does Dr. Neher vow to do in the future?

Mr. Kelley (not his real name) sits on the examination table, a collection of tics and spasms, refusing to meet my gaze. His obvious anxiety suggests that he is building up to some important disclosure. "You know," he finally says, looking out the window, "I've never told anybody about this. . . ." He clears his throat. "I was sexually abused as a kid."

I stare at him blankly a moment, his statement not registering. Then slowly, the enormity of what he just said starts to sink in. "I'm sorry to hear that," I tell him, knowing the words are inadequate. His revelation, however, instantly sheds a chilling light on his many and chronic peculiarities.

Unrecognized Indications

Ten years ago, I had welcomed him into my practice and took my first history and performed my first physical examination on him. At the time, he was in his early forties, with thinning red hair but a boyish, freckled face. Throughout his initial visit (and ever since), he avoided making eye contact and spoke only in short, nervous sentences. I noted in the chart that he had never married, and he reported no close friends. Although I was concerned about his social isolation, he seemed so acutely ill at ease that I thought it might actually be unkind to press for more details. I promised myself I would ask about it later, but never did.

Eight years ago, I found a small melanoma on his back. Mr. Kelley had accepted the news as if it was no consequence, as if the possibility of disfigurement or death was a mere annoyance. Fortunately, he did well medically. Mr. Kelley, I now understood, had already faced far greater challenges than skin cancer.

Four years ago, Mr. Kelley developed a rectal prolapse that required surgical repair. I asked him if he had any thoughts about why the condition might have developed. Mr. Kelley said only that he had a problem with chronic constipation.

That explanation seemed to be enough for the surgeon. I don't think the surgeon or I even considered the possibility of perineal injury.

Misdirected Anger

Back in the present, Mr. Kelley tugs at his collar and coughs. "I was fired from my job, too."

"When was that?" I ask.

"Last week."

Two years ago, Mr. Kelley had been injured at his job in a warehouse when he slipped on a wet floor and hurt his back. Although lumbar imaging showed only some arthritis and minor disk disease, his pain incapacitated him. The episode also unleashed from him a torrent of anger. As I filled out innumerable work capacity forms, white-hot rage poured out of him at my office. It poured out of him at the job site too, until everyone there became just a little afraid of him, marking him as the type of man who might just "go postal."

Part of his anger was directed at his injury and his work situation. But I knew the man well enough by now to suspect that, at its root, this rage went far deeper. I suggested that he see a counselor for anger management. Initially reluctant, he eventually followed through on the suggestion. Those anger management sessions must have been effective. He now knew with absolute certainty where his anger was coming from.

A Threat

"The abuse went on for years, you know," he adds. A sardonic grin flashes across his face. "I tracked him down on the Internet—found out that he's still alive. He's down in Rock Ridge . . . across the street from a grade school."

His personal darkness seems to close in around us. Mr. Kelley stiffens. "All I want to do now . . . is go down there and kill that bastard!" he spits.

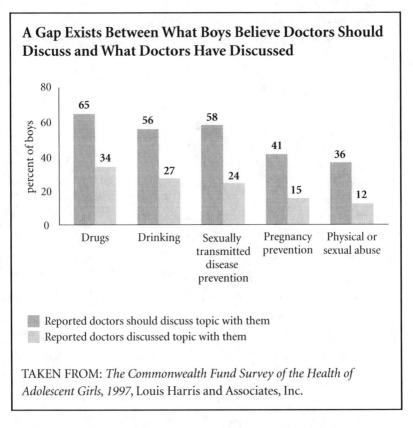

A Gap Exists Between What Boys Believe Doctors Should Discuss and What Doctors Have Discussed

percent of boys

	Drugs	Drinking	Sexually transmitted disease prevention	Pregnancy prevention	Physical or sexual abuse
Reported doctors should discuss topic with them	65	56	58	41	36
Reported doctors discussed topic with them	34	27	24	15	12

Reported doctors should discuss topic with them
Reported doctors discussed topic with them

TAKEN FROM: *The Commonwealth Fund Survey of the Health of Adolescent Girls, 1997,* Louis Harris and Associates, Inc.

I suddenly feel lost, not expecting and certainly not prepared for this. "Is that something you are planning to do, Mr. Kelley?" I ask, guessing that having a plan or purchasing a weapon might increase the likelihood of violence. Mr. Kelley shifts his gaze out the window again and does not answer. In a moment of near panic, I believe he might actually carry out his threat.

"You know it's not a good idea," I blurt out, not knowing if confrontation is the right thing to do. "In the long run, it won't make you any happier."

He sits silently for a long moment, his eyes focused somewhere far away. My pulse pounds in my ears as I watch his face intently. Finally, he takes a deep breath, looks down at the floor, and says, "No, I suppose not."

I relax a little, but I am not ready to trust that the situation has been diffused so quickly. "Is it all right with you if I call your anger management therapist and tell her about this?" I ask, extremely thankful that I have solid backup already in place.

Mr. Kelley squirms where he sits on the examination table, as if the thought of anyone else knowing makes him very uncomfortable. Finally, the internal struggle ends. "Sure, I guess. I guess that's okay."

"Good. Let me do that right now."

Regrets and a Vow

I step out of the room and a wave of fatigue causes me to sag against the wall. Intense emotions vie for recognition. I feel anger at the abuser, sorrow for Mr. Kelley, apprehension about his dangerous rage, and disbelief that we have been running circles around the central issue of this man's life for as long as I have known him.

I take a few slow, deep breaths and try to regain my composure. Was there any way of avoiding this crisis by getting to the truth sooner? Mr. Kelley's defenses had obviously been strong, but sadly, I realize I never asked any probing questions that might have helped him tell his story.

I push up from the wall, vowing to take more diligent and courageous social and sexual histories from now on. While I may not get a full account right away, I owe it to Mr. Kelley and every other hidden abuse survivor to at least start the conversation.

I need to make a phone call. With the right diagnosis, we can finally start the process of healing.

> "Eight months after he told this long-
> held secret . . . Eric shot himself. He
> was 29 years old."

Many Victims of Sexual Abuse by Priests Commit Suicide

Teresa Malcolm

Years after having been repeatedly sexually abused by his priest, Eric Patterson took his own life. In the emotional aftermath, his family was contacted by numerous parents of similar victims. Seeing a need, the Pattersons formed a support group for other family members of clergy sexual abuse survivors to help them deal with their feelings of betrayal by the Catholic Church and to demand accountability. Teresa Malcolm is a staff writer for the National Catholic Reporter.

As you read, consider the following questions:

1. What is the name of the Web site that the Pattersons have created?

2. What symptoms of sexual abuse did Eric exhibit?

3. What has happened to some parents who weren't quiet about the abuse of their children?

Since his teen years, Janet and Horace Patterson's son Eric had suffered from often debilitating depression. The family, including Eric's two sisters and a brother, struggled to understand the source of his intense psychological suffering. Even though the cloud would occasionally lift, when he would regain some control over his life and they could see Eric's best—compassionate and spiritual, intelligent and gifted with language—his illness would always return.

During Eric's second psychiatric hospitalization, his sister Becky questioned his idea of a vengeful God who could never be pleased, and asked if he had always felt that way. His answer: "No, it all changed when I was 12." That was when, he told her, he had been sexually abused by their priest. At the time he was an altar boy at St. Joseph Church in Conway Springs [Kansas].

Eight months after he told this long-held secret, on Oct. 29, 1999, Eric shot himself. He was 29 years old.

A Collection of Victims

In the five years since Eric's suicide, his parents have found themselves immersed in a cause they never would have expected: demanding accountability from the leaders of the Catholic Church for their handling of sexually abusive priests, and, for Janet Patterson especially, offering a listening ear, a source of support to victims and their families all over the United States.

Among those who have contacted her have been numerous families who have lost a loved one to suicide. Collected through those contacts and from news stories, she has a list of 145 victims of priest sexual abuse who have killed themselves.

Sexual Abuse of Minors by Priests and Deacons

The majority of allegations of sexual abuse were made against priests who were accused of having committed abusive acts more than one time. Only slightly more than one quarter (29%) of the allegations involve only a single instance of abuse.

Number of times abused, per victim

No. of times abused	Count	Percent
Once	2,759	29%
More than once	1,734	18.3%
Numerous times	5,002	52.7%
Total	9,493	100%

TAKEN FROM: *The Nature and Scope of the Problem of Sexual Abuse of Minors by Priests and Deacons,* by Karen Terry et al., prepared by the John Jay College of Criminal Justice (Washington DC: USCCB, 2004).

The Response

What was once Eric's bedroom is now the "War Room" in the Patterson home, where they run a Web site, "We Are Alert," answer e-mails and take phone calls. As Janet Patterson described it, "We're just a family sitting in the middle of a wheat field in the middle of America, and we lost a son to suicide because of clergy sexual abuse, and we're just trying to make sure it doesn't happen to other people." Patterson, 60, is retiring a year early from her job as a teacher at Conway Springs High School in order to devote her time to the sexual abuse survivor movement.

Her husband Horace, a 61-year-old technical writer, said, "I look at it as moving on with him, instead of moving on without him."

Support for Families

The Pattersons' work is taking a new turn with the planned formation of a support group for family members of clergy sexual abuse survivors. An initial meeting for the group is to be held in Denver at the June 11–13 [2004] national conference of the Survivors Network of those Abused by Priests, known as SNAP.

Outreach to family members is "long overdue," said David Clohessy, executive director of SNAP. "So much focus has been just on the individual victims. That doesn't even begin to scratch the surface of the betrayal and hurt."

Through the nationwide contacts Janet Patterson has made already, "she's making a long painful road towards recovery a little less painful, a little shorter for many," he said.

Speaking with others who have been through the same experience helps parents and other family members understand the behavior of the loved one who has been abused, Patterson said. The family was also educated by Eric's psychologist, who after his death explained the effects of sexual abuse that were reflected in Eric's symptoms—depression, eating disorders, loss of trust in others. "Once we lost Eric and began to be educated about the reality of sexual abuse, we said, 'Oh yeah, that's Eric,'" Patterson said. "Now I understand. I've heard Eric's story coming from so many people's mouths that I understand him better now that I did before his death."

The Family Betrayed

The family's pain is compounded by the fact that "there really are so few people to talk to who understand the whole dynamic. Not only have we lost a child, it was because of practicing our faith actively that our child was put in harm's way. And so the parents naturally feel that not only was their child betrayed, their whole family was betrayed."

The priest that Eric said abused him, Robert Larson, was removed from ministry by the Wichita diocese in 1988, after complaints against him dating as early as 1981. In 2000, he pleaded guilty to charges of sex abuse involving three former altar boys and a teenager he visited in jail. Larson is now serving a three- to 10-year sentence at the state prison in Lansing.

Larson has denied molesting Eric or four other former altar boys in the area who have committed suicide—Daniel Romey, Bobby Thompson, Gilbert Rodriguez and Paul Tafolla, whose families say they believe the four were abused by Larson.

Shattered Faith

None of the Pattersons attends a Catholic church anymore. Janet Patterson said the betrayal touches previous generations who helped build their local parish. "I think they have to be weeping in heaven." She noted that other parents have told her they have been ostracized by their parish community for speaking out about the abuse of their children.

One of the greatest effects on parents is an overwhelming guilt for what happened to their child. "I even felt guilty because we moved back from California to my hometown to keep our kids safe," Patterson said.

Clohessy said, "One benefit when parents talk to each other is people begin to cut through that misplaced shame and guilt and self-blame. It's easier to stop kicking yourself when you listen to other parents and realize they were all hoodwinked just the way I was."

At the first meeting for the family support group in Denver, Patterson hopes to have a psychologist speak about the effects of sexual abuse. The gathering will give family members a chance to share their stories. "By having as many parents as possible meeting in Denver," she said, "we hope to get a realistic idea of how best to set up support features and [what are] the primary needs of family members needing support."

"'I think what you need to do . . . to come out of it . . . is to first of all . . . admit to yourself that it wasn't your fault.'"

The Ability to Recover from Childhood Abuse Depends on Family and Community Support

Victoria L. Banyard and Linda M. Williams

Some teens who have been sexually abused go on to lead happy, productive lives; however, many do not. This viewpoint examines the resilience of abuse survivors, discussing risk factors and protective factors at the individual, family, and community levels. Victoria L. Banyard is a professor of Psychology at the University of New Hampshire and co-director of Prevention Innovations: Research and Practices for Ending Violence Against Women on Campus. Linda M. Williams is professor of Criminal Justice and Criminology at the University of Massachusetts and author of several publications on child and sexual abuse and family violence.

Victoria L. Banyard and Linda M. Williams, "Adolescent Survivors of Sexual Abuse: Developmental Outcomes," *The Prevention Researcher*, April 2007, vol. 14, no. 2, pp. 6–10. Copyright © 2007 Integrated Research Services, Inc. Reproduced by permission.

As you read, consider the following questions:

1. How does this viewpoint define sexual abuse?
2. According to the viewpoint, what can parents do to be protective factors and not risk factors in their teen's recovery from sexual abuse?
3. How can community programs support at-risk teens?

Sexual abuse can take many forms, from abuse within the family during childhood or adolescence to dating violence at the hands of an intimate partner or acquaintance. It is important to attend to these experiences because of the negative impact they can have on mental and physical health across the lifespan. However, not all youth who experience sexual victimization will have negative outcomes. Resilience, defined as positive development following adversity, is possible in the presence of resources both within individuals and their broader social context.... This article reviews research on key factors that put adolescent survivors of sexual abuse (defined as unwanted or inappropriate sexual contact whatever the victim's relationship to the perpetrator) at risk for negative developmental outcomes and on the resources that may enhance positive outcomes and recovery. Additionally, quotes from our qualitative work with adult women who experienced sexual abuse in childhood will be used to highlight opportunities for positive recovery....

Individual Level Variables

At the individual level, sexual abuse carries risk for shame and self-blame which can impact one's developing identity and which in turn have negative impacts on psychological functioning. It is also associated with a variety of physical and mental health concerns. Sexual abuse in childhood, for example, is associated with increased depression, posttraumatic stress symptoms, and anxiety. These relationships are complex, however, because of the fact that sexual abuse often does not occur in isolation but rather in combination with other forms of child maltreatment at the hands of family members or dating violence by intimate partners. The interaction of such experiences adds further to the web of risk presented by sexual violence; research using both adolescent and adult samples show clearly that experiencing multiple traumas is linked with more negative outcomes.

Individual Risk Factors

In addition to consequences for psychological development, sexual abuse also impacts behavior. While adolescence is a time of increased risk-taking in general, sexual victimization appears to add to rates of such behaviors. For example, [J.A.] Siegel and [L.M.] Williams found that survivors of childhood sexual abuse were more likely than a matched sample without official records of abuse to have been adjudicated as juveniles, particularly with arrests for violent crimes and running away. Other research has noted sexual abuse as a risk factor for prostitution. [C.R.] Browning and [E.O.] Laumann's empirical work show links between childhood sexual abuse and earlier onset of sexual activity in adolescence, increased numbers of sexual partners, and increased risk for sexually transmitted infections. Their research and others' also notes childhood sexual abuse as a risk factor for re-victimization, experiencing further sexual assaults in the teen or adult years. The idea is that sexual abuse creates a transition to a set of contexts in adolescence (e.g. contexts that create exposure to substance use or where there is little adult supervision) that carry greater risk for coming into contact with additional perpetrators who force sexual contact. Furthermore, in a community sample of adolescents, [V.L.] Banyard, [C.] Cross, and [K.] Modecki show sexual abuse in childhood is a risk factor for perpetrating dating violence among a sample of male and female adolescents.

Stories of Risk

We have conducted a qualitative study of narratives of child sexual abuse survivors who were interviewed as adults. Their stories map well onto the broader empirical findings related to risk and protective factors. One woman talked about adolescence as a period of risk for her:

> "... getting' high or getting' drunk or something like that, you know, to make the pain go away, ... an' it don't go nowhere ... I mean, that pain is still there ... that's how I realized I can't do drugs to get away with pain ... "

Sexual abuse in the context of dating violence in adolescence has similar negative consequences. For example, Banyard and Cross found links between dating violence and higher levels of depression and substance use as well as more negative attitudes toward school. [D.M.] Ackard and [D.] Neumark-Sztainer found date rape was associated with disordered eating behavior as well as mental health problems, including low self-esteem, for both boys and girls. Finally, analysis of the National Survey of Adolescents found sexual abuse (defined across incidents within and external to the family) linked to increased probability of co-occurring diagnoses of posttraumatic stress disorder, major depressive episode, and substance abuse.

Protective Factors

Numerous protective factors which help shield youth who have experienced sexual victimization from negative outcomes have also been identified at the intrapersonal or individual level of analysis. For example, [M.] Rutter's classic study outlines the key role of building self-esteem for children facing adversity and understanding how children think about what has happened to them. Other research on child sexual abuse survivors has highlighted the role of coping resources, though again, the majority of research has focused on adult survivors in this regard. These studies tend to find that survivors who report coping with their abuse by using avoidance strategies (e.g., tried not to think about it) also report more negative mental health outcomes. The exact impact of coping seems to depend on the type of coping survivors use to deal with the abuse itself, rather than the more general coping styles with which they approach a variety of stressors in their lives. In the words of a survivor of child sexual abuse describing her current coping with her abuse history:

> "I think what you need to do . . . to come out of it . . . is to first of all . . . admit to yourself that it wasn't your fault. Y'know, regardless if you had on scanty clothes, or . . . you in the wrong place at the wrong time. Nobody has a right . . . to touch you if you don't wanna be touched. Y'know. An' I think that's the first thing you have to do. So that you can try to . . . deal with the guilt and the shame. And the second thing you have to do is to empower yourself. Maybe even go to a group. Or maybe you can read, like I did.
>
> I, basically just . . . accepted the fact that that has happened to me, it's in the past. There's nothing I can do about it to change what happened. I'm just mentally picking myself up and dusting myself off . . . I can't let it get the best of me . . . like I'm in control of my life now."

Family Level Variables

Moving to other levels of the ecological model, family variables may also offer both areas of risk as well as protection and aid in the protective process that Rutter [in a 1987 publication] identifies as "reduction of risk impact." Research has particularly highlighted parental reactions to disclosure and the key role of social support. For example, in a recent qualitative study, children who disclosed sexual abuse noted the difficulty of finding times that were private enough to disclose and also described their acute sensitivity to the reactions of those whom they told. Overall, across this literature, which again tends to focus on adult survivors' retrospective reports, results show that disclosure is difficult and infrequent, that negative disclosure reactions from others has negative impacts on survivors' adjustment and recovery, while positive support whether during disclosure or afterward is a protective factor that promotes healing. Further, one study of adult survivors showed that longer delays before disclosing child sexual abuse were associated with greater trauma symptoms. These effects seem consistent whether the sexual abuse was in the context of family violence or as part of dating violence experienced in adolescence.

Additional risk at the family level may also be presented when child sexual abuse occurs within a broader context of family relationship dysfunction that carries risk for negative developmental outcomes among children. . . . Given the powerful role of early relationships in one's developing sense of self and trust in relationships with others, the negative impact of abuse on adolescents becomes clear. As [E.H.] Erickson notes, these are the key developmental tasks of adolescence and early adulthood—to develop a positive and coherent identity and positive relationships and intimacy with others. His theory would predict, then, that sexual abuse with its documented negative consequences in these domains, would create particularly problematic effects for teens with such experiences in their background. One survivor from our qualitative study had this to say:

> "Because it did happen to me so I never had a chance, 'cause I was so young . . . to experience men . . . another way. But I don't trust that man [meaning any man she might come in contact with]. . . . [I ask myself] well, how's that man, he might be the same way, I mean, . . . I don't even trust my own husband, and that's bad . . . he never gave me no reason not to . . . but, thing is . . . I just . . . fear it . . . don't want it to happen to my kids. I don't want 'em to go through something like that."

What to Do If a Child Discloses Sexual Exploitation

Don't

- Underreact to or minimize the information

- Overreact to the information or panic

- Criticize or blame the child

Do

- Respect the child's privacy

- Support the child and the decision to tell

- Show physical affection, and express love and support with words and gestures

- Explain to the child that he or she has done nothing wrong

- Help the child understand it was the offender's responsibility, not the child's

- Remember that children seldom lie about acts of sexual exploitation

- Keep the lines of communication open

- Seek appropriate medical care for the child

- Notify law enforcement

- Alert the child-protection, youth-services, child-abuse, or other appropriate social-services organizations in cooperation with law enforcement

National Center for Missing & Exploited Children,
http://www.missingkids.com/missingkids/servlet/
PageServlet?LanguageCountry=en_US&PageId=1486.

Family Protective Factors

Returning again to protective factors, one of the most consistent findings in the literature on resilience is the importance of supportive adult figures in the lives of children and teens. For example, [T.] Luster and [S.A.] Small showed the protective function of having parents who monitor and show an interest in adolescents friends and how they spend their time (parental monitoring) and parents who show caring and are fair with their teen (parental support). As one survivor noted:

> "When my parents said, 'What's the matter?' and I told them and then I slowed down and began being [myself]. . . . If [kids] are goin' through problems they ain't gonna come out and tell what problems they goin' through, they start getting' high. . . . I wish I had just sat down told my parents 'please listen to me' instead of runnin' to drugs and alcohol."

Another offered advice to girls who have experienced sexual abuse:

> "I would say don't hold it in. I would say that you, you have to speak on it. You have to talk about it because if you hold it in, it's going to fester and it's gonna hold you back in life."

Indeed, one participant talked directly about how she feels her mother tried to shelter her after the abuse, but part of that sheltering was not talking about what had happened. As a consequence this survivor never heard her mother say that what the perpetrator did to her was wrong. Thus, another survivor says:

> "First admit to themselves that it wasn't their fault. . . . And then try to work on the emotions that they've felt . . . [they] should talk to somebody, somebody that they can really really talk to and just let it out and not feel ridiculed, not have to worry about 'oh I can't say this and I can't say that.'"

Community Level Variables

Finally, [U.] Bronfenbrenner's model pushes us to also consider risk and protective factors at the broader community level. [R.] Campbell et al. examined the experiences of adult sexual assault survivors and their contact with community agencies including legal, medical, and mental health professionals. Posttraumatic stress symptoms were elevated among survivors who reported what they termed "secondary victimization" which consists of a variety of negative experiences including blaming attitudes by community professionals, not being given explanation about medical procedures, or being told the case was not serious enough to pursue. Though their research focuses on adults, it has important lessons for work with teens in highlighting how wrong steps taken by or problematic attitudes within communities can further exacerbate the risks associated with sexual abuse.

Community Protective Factors

However, communities, including schools, workplaces, and neighborhoods, are also a powerful source of protective processes. Rutter, for example, highlights the importance of protective processes including reducing further negative events that may follow from adversity, such as negative disclosure reactions and negative experiences with the criminal justice system. He also highlights the importance of "opening of opportunities" for survivors, including increasing the availability of resources and chances for promoting positive development. He specifically discusses the protective role of graduating from high school for some youth because of the other positive opportunities that milestone makes possible. Again, the experiences of survivors in our qualitative study are instructive. The majority of the 21 participants spontaneously described "turning points" in their lives, many of which were described as occurring during childhood or adolescence as a result of the intervention of a supportive adult or the assistance of a community program. In addition, during the interviews participants were asked what advice they would give to girls who experienced sexual abuse. One participant responded by focusing on the role of schools and education:

> "I would say, go get help. I never got help.... Somebody who cares about and you know talk about it, Stay off the street. Stay in school. Definitely stay in school. All my troubles happened when I used to hooky school and run away from home. There ain't nothing out there in them streets but trouble. I would say, get that education. I wish I did."

[B.] Hyman and [L.M.] Williams found that those who were sexually abused in childhood and completed high school were more resilient and were three times as likely to demonstrate economic resilience and less likely to be arrested or report substance abuse problems. In other research, several studies show that higher levels of perceived neighborhood support was a protective factor for teens who had experienced dating violence.

Communities can offer places for such opportunities for survivors whether through the availability of programs in schools to prevent further violence and educate young people about healthy relationships, support groups to promote healing, or opportunities for employment, recreation, and other activities that can support and build self-esteem. For example, schools are a potentially rich source of positive adult relationships and close friendships for teens as well as a place for building self-esteem through academic achievement or opportunities to learn new problem-solving skills. The workplace can offer mentoring and job skills which can help build self-esteem and a sense of self-efficacy. [K.] Bogenschneider outlines key ways community programs in general can support at-risk teens with many recommendations that are germane to sexual abuse survivors. For example, she lists the importance of facilitating positive school experiences, helping youth improve problem-solving and interpersonal skills, and developing a sense of social responsibility and strong community bonds. This work challenges us to think about opportunities for prevention and intervention not only at the individual level of the survivor but beyond to creating a more supportive community context for prevention and recovery. As one survivor in our qualitative study noted:

> "Go get that child some help. If that child is like 13, 14, 15 and your parents are not giving you no help, you go get your help yourself. Because there are places that you can go . . ."

What this review makes clear is that adolescents who have experienced sexual abuse, whether during childhood or adolescence, at the hands of family members or dating partners, are at particular risk for an array of negative outcomes not only for their mental and physical health, but also in relation to the particular developmental tasks of adolescence, those of identity formation and relationship building. Research suggests the need to reduce risk factors and bolster protective processes at all levels of the ecological model. This means that while individual treatment programs and prevention programs that alter specific behaviors are an important cornerstone of work in this area, the safety nets for survivors must be larger. The safety nets must include parents and other adult role models who are educated to be positive supports for survivors, schools as safe havens for building self-esteem and learning new and healthy ways to build relationships, and broader communities that empower children and teens rather than leaving them socially and politically powerless to change their situations. In this way all community members can play a role in supporting abused youth, responding to decrease the prevalence of sexual violence and to increase youth's resources for dealing with their own victimization.

Periodical Bibliography

The following articles have been selected to supplement the diverse views presented in this chapter.

AORN Journal	"Victims of Childhood Abuse Spend More on Health Care," vol. 87, no. 5, May 2008, p. 986.
Emily Bazelon	"A Question of Resilience," *The New York Times Magazine*, April 30, 2006, p. 54.
Bruce Bower	"Abused Kids React to Genetics, Adult Support," *Science News*, vol. 166, no. 21, November 20, 2004, p. 323.
Doug Brunk	"The True Incidence of U.S. Child Abuse Deaths Unknown: Fragmented Surveillance System Blamed," *Family Practice News*, vol. 34, no. 7, April 1, 2004, p. 82.
Child Welfare Information Gateway	"Long-Term Consequences of Child Abuse and Neglect," April 2008. www.childwelfare.gov/pubs/factsheets/long_term_consequences.pdf.
Bob Herbert	"Children in Torment," *The New York Times*, March 9, 2006, p. A23.
Teena M. McGuinness and Kristina Schneider	"Poverty, Child Maltreatment and Foster Care," *American Psychiatric Nurses Association Journal*, vol. 13, no. 5, October 2007, pp. 296–303.
National Scientific Council on the Developing Child	"Excessive Stress Disrupts the Architecture of the Developing Brain," Working Paper No. 3, 2005. http://www.developingchild.net/pubs/wp/Stress_Disrupts_Architecture_Developing_Brain.pdf.
Virginia J. Noland, Karen D. Liller, Robert J. Murdoch, Martha L. Coulter, and Ann E. Seraphine	"Is Adolescent Sibling Violence a Precursor to College Dating Violence?" *American Journal of Health Behavior*, vol. 28, supplement 1, 2004, pp. S13–S23.

OPPOSING
VIEWPOINTS®
SERIES

How Can Child Abuse Be Prevented?

Chapter Preface

No one really knows how many children in the United States suffer from some form of child abuse each year, because many cases go undetected or unreported. Estimates are wide ranging: 903,000 verified cases in 2002; more than 800,000 cases in 2005; one in twenty-five children in 2000; and three to four deaths per day from abuse or neglect in 2000. In 2005, one study estimated as many as five in twenty-five children are abused if the numbers of unreported cases are factored into the total.

Although exact numbers are difficult to determine, some experts estimate that elementary classroom teachers are in contact with at least five to ten abused children per ten years of teaching. And the estimates are higher for middle and high school teachers. Child-educators, along with other professionals such as clergy, doctors, nurses, police, and psychotherapists, are in a unique position to act as a bridge between families and the community. Educators can identify and report cases of abuse and connect children and families to the help they need.

In fact, in all fifty states certain professionals, such as teachers, clergy, and doctors, are legally required to report suspected abuse. If professionals know what to look for and how to report suspected cases, they can help improve or even save a child's life.

With futures and lives at stake, mandatory reporting is generally regarded as a good thing, but not everyone agrees. The system is set up to err on the side of false identifications in an effort to ensure that no legitimate cases fall through the cracks. Not only are teachers and others *required* to immediately report all suspected cases of abuse, but in some states they could face penalties (including the loss of professional licenses, civil law suits, hefty fines, and even imprisonment) if they do not report suspected cases of abuse. In fact, the 903,000 cases verified in 2002 are from five million reported cases, and the more than 800,000 cases in 2005 stem from 3.3 million reported cases involving more than six million children. Annually, reports indicate that only about one quarter of all reported cases are substantiated. In 2005, 40 percent of all reports did not, according to state workers, even merit an investigation. Furthermore, in some investigated cases children are removed from their families and their parents are charged and incarcerated only to be found not-guilty later.

Faults in the system arguably result in children being unnecessarily traumatized and families being destroyed. On the other hand, many actual cases of child abuse go undetected or unreported. Still other cases are reported and should be investigated but are not. Horrific cases of children tortured, severely neglected, and even murdered make national news headlines every year.

Is it really in the best interest of families and these professionals to require that all suspected instances of child abuse be reported? There are arguments for both viewpoints. This chapter discusses different sides of several approaches to preventing and reducing child abuse.

> *"A 35-year-old man who came to me had started as a nine-year-old. By the time I saw him he had abused more than 500 children."*

Early Intervention Can Prevent Sexual Abusers Who Are Children from Becoming Pedophiles

Angela Neustatter

Many sexual abusers of children start offending as adolescents or children themselves. According to this viewpoint, most children who are abusers have had shocking childhood experiences from which they need to heal, and society needs to recognize this instead of writing them off as monsters who cannot possibly change. Fortunately, programs with intense therapy for these young offenders are producing promising results. Angela Neustatter is a journalist, author, and lecturer in journalism.

As you read, consider the following questions:

1. What percentage of people convicted of sexual abuse are under the age of twenty?

2. According to a three-year study of 280 identified juvenile sexual abusers, at what age did they begin to abuse?

3. Why does Eileen Vizard believe that we cannot overstress the importance of taking the acts of young abusers seriously?

Kay will never know whether reporting her 14-year-old son Jon to social services for sexually abusing a neighbour's child prevented him from moving on to become an adult paedophile in the style of Ian Huntley and Roy Whiting. Would he have been another Chris Langham, who was last week [August 2007] found guilty of downloading sadistic and depraved child pornography? Or a Timothy Cox, recently put inside on an indeterminate sentence for running an internet chat room where punters watched filmed abuse of children, including the rape of babies?

It is certainly possible, says Donald Findlater, deputy director of the Lucy Faithfull Foundation, where he works therapeutically with paedophiles. He hears time and again how their abusing began when they were children: "A 35-year-old man who came to me had started as a nine-year-old. By the time I saw him he had abused more than 500 children."

Such revelations rarely make us question what leads a nine-year-old boy to do this, but increase the cry for ever more punitive measures to deal with adult offenders. Earlier this year the government raised the possibility of chemical castration. While Kate McCann and her husband must face the fact that child abduction and trafficking is one way that children end up appearing in the kind of pornography watched by Langham.

But we ignore the fact that the child may be the father of the adult paedophile. Twenty per cent of people convicted of sexual offences are under the age of 20, according to the Home Office. Victim surveys report that 30–50 per cent of child sex abuse is carried out by young children and adolescents. Some 50 per cent of adult sexual offenders report sexual deviance in adolescence.

Paedophiles do not just appear fully formed as adults, says Andrew Durham, who works with child sex abusers for Warwickshire Council. "But fear and loathing of paedophiles blocks people from understanding the importance of their childhood circumstances. There is always something in childhood that breaks down the moral compass, in my experience. Many feel inadequate and isolated misfits who cannot form relationships with their peers. They gain power and control through abuse of younger children."

Preventing more victims lies at the heart of the work of Eileen Vizard, consultant child and adolescent psychiatrist and clinical director of the NSPCC's National Child Assessment and Treatment Service. For more than 20 years she has researched, diagnosed and treated some of the country's most disturbed and dangerous children who are sexually abusing others and who, if not helped to stop, may be on a trajectory that will lead to compulsive abusing as an adult.

Vizard led and co-authored the recently published first major study into this phenomenon, entitled *Links Between Juvenile Sexually Abusive Behaviour and Emerging Severe Personality Disorder Traits in Childhood*. It was funded by the Home Office and published on their website in November last year [2006].

Early Difficulties

This is a three-year study of 280 identified juvenile sexual abusers, more than 90 per cent male. Abusing had very occasionally begun as young as at five-and-a-half years, although 14 years was average. More than half had abused victims five years younger than themselves and the majority abused female victims. There are great similarities in the behaviour of young abusers and adult offenders. Most had abused relatives, friends and acquaintances. In more than half the cases there had been penetration, masturbation and oral sex; one-third used verbal coercion. In some cases there had been co-abusers.

The extent and reality of child-on-child sex abuse is shocking, but so are the childhood experiences and circumstances child abusers endure. Without exception, they share childhoods that should not be tolerated in a caring society.

A quarter endured physical abuse, 74 per cent emotional abuse, 71 per cent sexual abuse; 92 per cent were exposed to domestic violence and 73 per cent experienced family breakdown. Nearly half were found to have "inadequate sexual boundaries." The research divided juvenile sexual abusers into "early onset"—those beginning before the age of 11—and "late onset" beginning after this age. The first group were more likely to have experienced inadequate family sexual boundaries; multiple forms of abuse, poor parenting and insecure attachment. The latter group misused substances, targeted specific groups and often used verbal coercion.

Vizard sees a "developmental trajectory" where the abusers may be having sexual fantasies and beginning harmful behaviour towards other children. She says: "Without help, some sexualised children may move on to abusing other children at home or at school, later masturbating to sexual images of children and becoming entrenched in patterns of frank sexual abuse of children."

The Internet Factor

The research also shows a sub-group with emerging severe personality disorder who are more likely to have an early difficult temperament; more insecure attachment; inconsistent parenting; placement disruption and parents with mental health problems. Their sexual abusing is often premeditated and predatory. The fear that child abusing may increase through the stimulus of online child pornography which more and more children and young people access is chillingly real.

What Are Warning Signs of Sexually Harmful or Abusive Behavior?

Behaviors that may indicate increased risk include. . .

- Regularly minimizing, justifying, or denying the impact of inappropriate behaviors on others.

- Making others uncomfortable by consistently missing or ignoring social cues about others' personal or sexual limits and boundaries.

- Preferring to spend time with younger children rather than peers.

- Insisting on physical contact with a child even when that child resists.

- Responding sexually to typical gestures of friendliness or affection.

- Reluctance to be alone with a particular child; becoming anxious when a particular child is coming to visit.

- Offering alcohol/drugs, sexual material or inappropriate "privileges" to younger child.

Stronger indicators of risk for abusive behavior include. . .

- Linking sexuality and aggression in language or behavior; engaging in sexually harassing behavior online or in person; and forcing any sexual interaction.

Stop It Now! "Do Children Sexually Abuse Other Children?
Preventing Sexual Abuse Among Children and Youth,"
www.stopitnow.org/downloads/Do_Children_Abuse.pdf.

The web features in half the cases of child-on-child sex abuse cases that Andrew Durham sees each year. "When young people see adults abusing children on the net, it normalises what is being done," he says.

The Taith Project, managed by Barnardo's, gets referrals of eight- to 18-year-olds from across Wales with "concerning" sexual behaviour. Denise Moultrie, the children services manager, says: "Particularly worrying about chat rooms is not just the images of child pornography being seen but the relationships children get into online around what they see."

Abusers Are Victims

The importance of taking the acts of young abusers seriously cannot be overstressed, says Vizard, who believes that as a society we have to do better than merely condemn paedophiles as depraved monsters as though they existed outside normal humanity; we have to understand how damaging their childhoods can be.

This is not indulgent liberalism, but a conviction, built on many years of learning how young abusers think, feel and behave, that potential victims could be protected by the kind of work that she and others are doing. What is needed is sufficient public support to ensure that the funding is made available to do this work on the scale that is needed.

Moultrie stresses that we are talking about children right across the social scale: "I think we are hugely handicapped in getting support because of public revulsion. A lot of professionals don't want to acknowledge that children are sexual abusers of other children. Parents read newspapers and don't want to identify their child as a monster, so they may reject the child or deny what is happening." Others, who might be prepared to support funding for children who are being abused, do not recognise that young people who are abusing other children may also need support.

Constructive Help

Yet Vizard has seen how, with intense therapy, young abusers change direction. Their disturbing and distorting experiences are addressed; they are helped to see why the way they are acting is wrong and the impact they have on victims. They are taught techniques based on cognitive behavioural therapy for dealing with feelings and impulses in a non-damaging way, rather than leaving them to develop the compulsive behaviour that makes adult paedophiles so very dangerous.

Durham is confident that working with young abusers makes a difference: "You can get remorse at what the victim has suffered. These young may not have reached the stage of blocking out empathy and they are capable of forming a relationship with me as a safe adult. So they will listen and see that they can choose to learn not to follow the path they have taken. We have been going 12 years and have a very low rate of repeat sexual offences."

Kay is one of an increasing number of mothers of teenagers who tell the Stop It Now! helpline—set up for those who are abusing or fear they may—about their problem. She says that reporting Jon was agonisingly difficult, but through his treatment, in which she was involved, he learned techniques for controlling his behaviour.

"We have learned to communicate as a family and to talk about whether a situation is 'safe' for him. He has a therapist and I feel so very grateful that through this work Jon has taken responsibility for changing."

But if that constructive help had not been available, she dreads to think what might have happened.

"*Teaching students parenting skills may be the most cost-effective way to reduce violent and abusive behaviors and prevent the transfer of violent behaviors from generation to generation.*"

Education Programs for Emotionally and Behaviorally Impaired Teens Can Prevent Child Abuse

Catherine Roberts, Clara Wolman, and Judy Harris-Looby

Concerned teachers and counselors of teen students with emotional and behavioral disorders (EBD) incorporated a parental training program, Project Baby Care, into their classrooms. In addition to a traditional reading and writing component, the course featured a practical part: During class, students took turns caring for two lifelike, computerized baby-dolls. At the end of the program, students demonstrated that they had increased their parenting skills, were less likely to use corporal punishment, and were more empathetic toward children. Catherine Roberts,

Catherine Roberts, Clara Wolman, and Judy Harris-Looby, "Project Baby Care: A Parental Training Program for Students with Emotional and Behavioral Disorders (EBD)," *Childhood Education*, Winter 2004/2005, vol. 81, pp. 101–103. Copyright © 2004/2005 by the Association for Childhood Education International. Reproduced by permission of the Association for Childhood Education International, 17904 Georgia Avenue, Suite 215, Olney, MD.

Clara Wolman, and Judy Harris-Looby are full-time faculty in the Graduate Exceptional Education Program at Barry University in Miami Shores, Florida.

As you read, consider the following questions:

1. How much did this program cost?
2. How much more likely are teens with early onset psychiatric disorders to parent a child while still a teen?
3. Why was it especially disturbing that two of the students did not want to even touch the doll baby, ignored it, or demonstrated hatred toward it?

The rate of reported child abuse fatalities has risen annually, with an estimated 1,400 child fatalities from abuse occurring in 2002 alone; even so, recent studies estimate that 50–60 percent of deaths from child abuse are not recorded. Whiplash and other symptoms of shaken baby syndrome (SBS) were reported as the cause of death in 17 percent of fatal child abuse cases.

A Special Need

Statistics indicate that many victims of such abuse are children of teenage parents. Parenting classes could lessen the prevalence of the problem, but such classes are under-utilized in this era of high-stakes testing. In particular, school curricula in special education do not adequately prepare students with special needs, particularly those with the most violent behaviors, for their most demanding job—parenting. Profiles of typical abuse perpetrators match the characteristics of many students with emotional and behavioral disorders (EBD) and place them at higher risk of acting impulsively and using violent and abusive behaviors; also, aggressive at-risk young men are more likely than other men to use harmful parenting strategies with their children. Newspapers continue to report child fatalities from SBS and other abuses by teenagers with EBD.

The Program

Teaching students parenting skills may be the most cost-effective way to reduce violent and abusive behaviors and prevent the transfer of violent behaviors from generation to generation. For less than $1,000, Project Baby Care, a parental training program developed and adapted for adolescents with EBD, proved successful in increasing their parental knowledge and skills and improving their attitudes toward caring for an infant. The curriculum used in this project included two main components: 1) a practical component of hands-on experiences involving the interaction of students with computerized doll-babies, and 2) a traditional component of reading, writing, and watching films.

The Students

Thirty-seven adolescents with emotional and behavioral disorders (EBD) participated in this project. These students had been assessed by a multidisciplinary committee as having emotional and behavioral problems that were severe enough to warrant placement in four self-contained classes in an urban educational center in southeast Florida. The participants included 24 males and 13 females, roughly evenly divided between Hispanic and black students (African Americans and Haitians). The ages of the students in each class ranged from 14 to 20 years. Fifty-four percent of the students were known to the courts, including 50 percent of all participating males and 62 percent of all participating females. Seventy percent of all the participants had been victims of recorded child abuse and/or neglect. Of the total number of participants, 63 percent of the males and 85 percent of the females had suffered child abuse and/or neglect. Seven female students who attended this program were mothers or pregnant at the time of data collection; two of these students were already mothers for the second time, and a third student with one child was pregnant with her second. Only four of the 24 boys had admitted fathering babies. This population is consistent with the data indicating that early onset of psychiatric disorders is associated with subsequent teen pregnancy among both males and females at a 33 percent greater rate than for other teens.

The curriculum included both practical and traditional reading and writing components.

Practical Component

The interactive program in this project used two computerized life-size doll-babies that realistically simulated infant behavior (purchased from Baby Think It Over, Inc.) The two doll-babies used in this project were a light-skinned African American boy baby, and a Hispanic girl baby. Each doll-baby has a realistic head that requires support. The lifelike baby has a 21-inch long vinyl body, weighs approximately 6–7 pounds, and is anatomically correct. Each doll needs to be cared for by the student in very realistic, concrete ways: through feeding, burping, cuddling, and diapering. Each doll-baby has an internal computer that is programmed to cry at random intervals and/or when the doll's head is not being properly supported. As positive feedback, the baby coos and burps when the student provides proper handling.

Observed Babysitting

On average, each session of actual class instruction with a doll-baby lasted over 60 minutes, four times per week. The lifelike baby was used in various hands-on activities (e.g., changing the diaper). For added realism, participants were required to care for the baby while completing their class work. The internal computer was programmed to affect the baby's behavior (e.g., simulating a calm baby or a fussy baby). This feature allowed the teachers and counselors to adjust and tailor stressors in the environment, and to observe the students' reactions and strategies used in response. Students who mishandled the doll-baby were readily identified by the doll's loud, continuous cry. The internal computers detected and signaled the doll to cry if students failed to support the doll's head, neglected the doll, and/or roughly handled the doll. The computers produced perceptually louder and longer crying if the baby was shaken.

Students interacted with the doll-babies only in the controlled setting of the classroom, and only when under observation by a counselor and at least one teacher during each session. The limitation of having only one doll-baby per session for the 10 or 11 students in each class placed some time limitations on total parenting time with the doll-babies.

Reading and Writing (Traditional) Component

The curriculum was adapted from a project called the Nurturing Program for Teenage Parents and Their Families. This project also used a series of paperback books called *The Parent Guidebooks for Growing Families*. The latter were particularly useful in teaching students who were non-readers or very low readers the appropriate expectations for the stages of infant development; the series has excellent graphics that facilitated reading. Films also were used.

Adapting the Program

The researchers adapted both components of the program to better serve the EBD population. The program was written on a 5th- and 6th-grade reading level, although the content interest was geared for adolescent/young adult interests. Modeled behaviors included: additional, repetitive activities, such as rocking the baby when it continued to cry; proper car-seat positioning; increased use of discussions and group counseling sessions (e.g., strategies to prevent frustration when the baby continued to cry); proactive methods of discipline (e.g., re-direction techniques, time-outs); creative role-playing (e.g., telling your parent you are going to be a parent, scenarios on being a single parent); and preparation of materials at a lower reading level, when needed.

Project Baby Care was included as part of the required Life Skills Management course. Each student received a grade for the 20-session course. Six current teachers at the center provided major support for this project. At the conclusion of the project, students in all four classes attended an awards ceremony and pizza party in recognition of their efforts to become better parents.

The researchers provided the curriculum to teachers in the program. Two overriding concepts were integral to all aspects of the curriculum: 1) discipline, don't hit the child, and 2) talk to and play with the child. One meeting was held with the teachers to review the program, stress the program's two main concepts, and discuss instructional strategies and their implementation. Training was not necessary, as the curriculum was self-explanatory and the teachers were already trained and competent in working with this special needs population. All program materials (e.g., films, lessons, books, pamphlets) were located in the office and available to the staff.

The Counselors

The efforts of the counselors associated with the program greatly enhanced its effectiveness. As part of their general duties, counselors were encouraged to observe the students in their assigned classes and initiate group activities. Their presence and the varied roles they played during the intervention increased its effectiveness. They were present in the classes during each scheduled lesson to encourage class discussions, field questions, observe inappropriate or abusive behaviors, and provide psychological support. Many of the topics led the students to recall past experiences that, in some instances, were upsetting; the counselors provided a comfort zone for the students. Requests for private counseling sessions were immediately honored.

Shaken Baby Syndrome

Shaken baby syndrome is the medical term used to describe the injuries resulting from shaking an infant or young child. Introduced in medical literature in 1972, shaken baby syndrome occurs when a child is shaken violently as part of an adult or caregiver's pattern of abuse or because an adult or caregiver momentarily succumbs to the frustration of having to respond to a crying baby. . . .

In shaken baby syndrome, the sudden and repeated vigorous shaking pitches the infant or child's brain in different directions and causes parts of the brain to pull away, tearing brain cells and blood vessels. The force of shaking a child in anger and frustration is five to 10 times greater than if the child were to simply trip and fall. That force is repeated in succession as the child is being shaken.

Violent shaking is especially dangerous to infants and young children because their neck muscles are not fully developed and their brain tissue is exceptionally fragile. Their small size further adds to their risk of injury.

Often, the outward signs of injury to an infant or young child are not obvious, as the injuries occur on the inside, particularly in the head or behind the eyes.

"Shaken Baby Syndrome," American Humane Association,
www.americanhumane.org.

Potential Abuse

During the sessions, counselors and staff noted certain anomalies. A few students refused to touch the doll-baby at all, and showed either total disregard or outright hatred for the baby, especially when it cried. All but one of these students were male. More important, two of these students resided in homes with younger siblings; one of these students resided with a sibling under 5 years old. A few other students appeared to abuse the doll-babies (i.e., tossing the baby, pulling the baby, twisting the skin of the baby, and shaking the baby) or tried to ignore it (refusing to hold the baby). In all but one instance, these abusive behaviors appeared when the students were unable to stop the doll-babies from crying. Only once did a male student initiate aggression against a quiet doll-baby. It is important to note that other students in the class immediately showed indignation and reported the incident to the counselor, teachers, and other students. On two occasions, this type of incident almost caused a fight as a student went to protect the doll-baby from another student's inappropriate behavior. Counselors added additional sessions of private counseling for those participants who exhibited abusive and/or neglectful behaviors. Also, they spoke with parents, guardians, and foster parents about participants' exhibited inappropriate behaviors. In two instances, a family social worker was assigned to the home.

A Real Situation

A more serious incident occurred with one of the students who already had a baby. Apparently, the student was leaving her 2-year-old at the homes of various people (not family) for weeks at a time so she could continue her social life. Counselors had to intervene when one of the people who was caring for the baby refused to release the baby to the student. The baby was finally released and the counselor contacted Family Services; a social worker was assigned to the case to monitor the household to ensure that the 2-year-old was being properly cared for. In addition, the student was required by the court to place the child in child care.

The Results

Before and after the project (pre- and posttest), students were administered two questionnaires: The Adult Adolescent Parenting Inventory and Test Your Nurturing Knowledge. The results showed that this program was very effective in three areas:

Knowledge About Parenting and Parenting Skills

This construct on knowledge about parenting reflects an understanding of the different stages of growth and development of a child, and the skills needed in the care and nurturing of a child. Comparison of pre- and posttest scores showed a strong increase in knowledge about parenting and parenting skills. Participants who were already parents were more knowledgeable than others before the project started but still gained additional knowledge from the curriculum intervention on parenting.

Beliefs About [Not] Using Corporal Punishment with Children

The students' beliefs about [not] using corporal punishment with children showed the greatest positive change as a result of this project. High post-intervention scores on this belief indicate that participants value alternatives to corporal punishment, refute the need for physical force, consider democratic rule-making that includes all family members, and respect children's needs as part of a mutual parent-child relationship. Success in reducing the belief of an at-risk EBD population in the necessity of using corporal punishment to discipline children was a primary goal of this study.

Empathy for the Child's Needs

Empathy refers to the ability of a person to be concerned about the needs and feelings of another. Empathic parents are sensitive to the needs of their children and create nurturing environments conducive to the intellectual, emotional, and social growth of their children. The authors observed increases from pre- to posttest scores in the students' empathy. This significant growth in awareness of children's needs indicated that the techniques used in the curriculum to increase empathic attitudes were effective.

A Success

This study demonstrated that students with EBD can be successfully trained in appropriate parenting skills. Sixty-eight percent of the surveyed students stated that the Project Baby Care program had helped them to recognize that "parenthood brought dramatic life changes" and were now aware of how unrealistic their expectations about their abilities to parent had been.

Most important, this program significantly reduced students' beliefs in the need for corporal punishment. During the program, they learned more effective and humane ways to discipline a child.

A parenting curriculum aimed at strengthening competencies and coping resources in an EBD population can provide a proactive approach to successful transition into adulthood and promote positive life skills.

"To date, no agency has been established
to investigate and respond to cases of
acquaintance abuse."

Adequately Screening Adults in Child-Serving Occupations Prevents Child Sexual Abuse

Monica Applewhite

Beginning with 1922, this viewpoint highlights the history of reported child abuse cases and how specific child-serving organizations and government agencies have responded. The author discusses the prevalence, yet the lack of attention paid to sexual abuse perpetrated by acquaintances, including priests and schoolteachers, and asserts that organizations must be constantly proactive because this type of abuse will always exist. Monica Applewhite is the president of the Religious Services Division of Praesidium, Inc. During the past 15 years she has conducted root-cause analysis of more than 1,100 cases of sexual abuse in child-serving organizations and has developed prevention and response systems.

Monica Applewhite, "Putting Abuse in Context," *America*, September 25, 2006, vol. 195, no. 8, pp. 14–16. Copyright © 2006 America Press, Inc. All rights reserved. Reproduced by permission.

As you read, consider the following questions:

1. In the 1970s, which child-serving nonprofit organization developed processes and procedures to lessen the risk of child sexual abuse occurring within their organization?

2. In 2000, how many reported cases of abuse of children by schoolteachers were reported in a six-month period?

3. What percentage of sexual abuse of children six years old or younger is committed by juvenile offenders?

When reports began to surface within the Boy Scouts of America that a male nurse was touching scouts inappropriately during overnight camping trips, the executive leadership, not pleased, replaced the nurse. Later, however, his replacement was removed after similar allegations. Confused and deeply disappointed that trusted, professional men could behave in a manner so contrary to scouting principles, the leadership resolved to prevent future incidents through more careful screening. That was in 1922.

Today when Catholics hear the term "sexual abuse," most of us consider our church's situation—the news reports about members of the clergy accused or convicted of abusing minors and the people at work who ask us, So are you still Catholic? "Abusive" does not describe the way we think of our faith or our church as a whole, or even the way we think of the wholesome priests whom we loved as children or befriend as adults.

I have worked in the field of organizational sexual abuse for more than 15 years, and I am still Catholic. Our church's experiences over the past few years have not discouraged me. It is not that I am naive; I understand the mistakes we have made. Having conducted hundreds of interviews with those who have perpetrated and experienced sexual abuse, including clergymen and their victims, I know the realities of sexual abuse. But my work has allowed me to know the problem in a much wider context than one can glean from the standard press reports.

Early Preventive Efforts

During the 1950's, the F.B.I. funded a public-awareness program to prevent sexual abuse of children. Preventing sexual abuse was simple: kids should not talk to strangers and should not take candy from strangers. The program focused on "Stranger Danger" and featured images of a shadowed man, hiding behind a tree with his hat pulled down, waiting for an innocent child to walk by. The campaign appealed to the American public. It was simple: there are good guys and bad guys.

Our first child-abuse reporting laws, passed in the 1960's, required human service professionals and ordinary citizens to report abuse if they knew about it. Before then, it was considered meddling in family business to report, known or suspected abuse to the police. Now, for the first time, law enforcement established protective services divisions to manage the cases of alleged abuse and to protect children by supervising families and, at times, removing children from homes.

Protective services did not, however, manage cases of "acquaintance abuse," that is, abuse perpetrated by known and trusted adults who are not members of the child's family. To date, no agency has been established to investigate and respond to cases of acquaintance abuse. Extremely complicated and difficult to understand, acquaintance abuse cases, until recently, did not fit within the public's understanding of sexual abuse.

Big Brothers

In 1974, Big Brothers of America, an organization with a mission to mentor at-risk youth, discovered that they had become a magnet for adults who were seeking sexual contact with children. Cases of adult sexual offenders who sought positions as big brothers began to emerge across the country.

Faced with this situation, Big Brothers had a decision to make: it could either shut down its program because it had become risky, or it could develop safe methods for fulfilling its mission. The organization chose to continue its work. It required in-depth screening, created new ways of supervising staff and volunteers and developed a system for questioning children and their parents about where a big brother took them on outings and what activities they selected. Today Big Brothers continues its high-risk work, while screening, selecting, monitoring and supervising individuals in one-on-one relationships with young people.

Why did the organization opt to continue, rather than to quit or change the program to disallow individual relationships?

When you talk with the leaders of Big Brothers about the choice, you find that they decided the risk was worth it. They realized that there is no substitute for the difference a relationship can make in the life of a child. So they continue, despite the challenges.

Big Brothers went a step further by asking other major volunteer organizations that served children to join with them to create abuse-prevention programs. They were met with polite refusals and denial ("Sorry to hear about your situation, but we don't really have a problem with that"). While Big Brothers embraced the complexity of its work and emerged as an organizational leader in preventing sexual abuse, it could only change itself.

The 1980s: Lawsuits and the Internet

During the 1980's, some youth-serving organizations were sued in civil courts for failing to prevent and properly respond to allegations of sexual abuse. When the claims increased in volume and intensity, youth camps, Y.M.C.A.'s, and Boys and Girls Clubs implemented abuse-prevention programs, which typically required staff to sign agreements to report abuse and to complete training, in which they learned the profile of a child molester and the indicators of abuse in children.

In the public sector, preventing sexual abuse meant teaching assertiveness skills to children. If someone touched them in a way that made them uncomfortable, children were taught to yell, "Stop!" and run away. By 1985 most public schools had programs to teach elementary school children how to "protect themselves" from sexual abuse.

During that same decade, a community of adults with a primary sexual attraction to minors started using the newly developed Internet to organize themselves. Today there are hundreds of Web sites and chat rooms where adults who are attracted to minors meet and discuss how to cultivate relationships with kids. The pervasive philosophy of these Internet communities is that children are sexual beings from the day they are born and that children, like adults, have a right to express their sexuality. If society did not disapprove, they believe, then children would not be harmed.

Every day on these sites adults who are attracted to minors talk about love and relationships, tell funny stories about the interesting, intelligent things their young friends say and reflect on how beautiful and special they are. They talk about helping children with their homework and teaching them to pitch a baseball. They believe they are helping kids who do not get enough attention at home or do not have enough food or new clothes. These adults seem to have an unending supply of time and attention. They are not strangers to the children they discuss, nor are they unimportant in the children's lives. As appealing as it may be, the idea of teaching children to yell "No!" when sexual contact is introduced by someone they love is perhaps more complicated than we would like to admit.

The Current Era

In March 2000, a small independent school district in Texas was struggling with a difficult situation. A male schoolteacher was caught with his hands inside the pants of a 9-year-old student, a little boy. The school district's response was first to

---

Sexual Abuse of Students

	Percent of Students Who Are Targets of Educator Sexual Misconduct		Percent of All Students in Sample	
	Male	Female	Male	Female
Caucasian	24.7	26.8	28.1	30.5
African Descent	10.1	15.2	9.2	10.6
Latina/o	5.1	10.6	5.2	7.2
American Indian	1.5	1.5	0.5	0.4
Asian	0.0	0.5	1.6	1.0
No Response	1.5	2.5	2.4	3.3
Total	42.9	57.1	47	53

TAKEN FROM: U.S. Department of Education, Office of the Under Secretary, *Educator Sexual Misconduct: A Synthesis of Existing Literature*, Washington, D.C., 2004.

---

transfer him to a school filled with minority students whose parents did not speak English. Then, after a similar incident, he was caught again and sent by the school district to a school for children with mental retardation. When he was caught a final time, the superintendent told him that if he would just go away quietly and leave the area, no further action would be taken against him. He was never arrested. When the superintendent was asked why he did not call the police, he said he feared that if he reported the incidents, a newspaper reporter could find out, and he did not want the name of the school reported in the paper.

That year newspapers around the country told of 244 reported cases of sexual abuse of children (alleged and convicted) perpetrated by schoolteachers over a six-month period. In large-scale studies of sexual abuse in schools, we find that about 10 percent of children in public schools have experienced an incident or an attempted abuse by the time they are 18 years old. About 40 percent of the cases in school involved female schoolteachers who initiate sexual contact with students.

In 2002 in New Jersey, a 43-year-old female schoolteacher was sentenced to probation instead of time in prison after confessing to having sexual contact with a 13-year-old boy. The judge's reported rationale for the probationary sentence was that "something had just clicked" between the teacher and the student. Yet studies on the effects of abuse by female perpetrators show that while victims often feel they were not abused, both the short-term and the long-term effects are virtually the same and in some cases more dramatic than when the perpetrator is a male. Women commit sexual abuse too.

So do children and young people. About 45 percent of sexual abuse of children 6 years old and under is perpetrated by juvenile offenders, many of them female.

These facts are difficult for us to fathom. Sexual abuse perpetrated by a person we know to be loving and kind is almost impossible to consider. Both current and retrospective studies show, however, that abuse by trusted adults who are not related to the child accounts for approximately 60 percent of the sexual abuse of children in our nation. Despite these findings, the problem of acquaintance abuse has been widely neglected by the criminal justice system and social services. Public service announcements and sexual-abuse-awareness programs rarely have the resources or time with participants to communicate the more complicated aspects of sexual abuse. As a result, funding to prevent acquaintance abuse has come almost exclusively from private, nonprofit, youth-serving organizations that are responding to their own need to manage risk.

The Catholic Church Crisis

In this environment, reports about sexual abuse in the Archdiocese of Boston emerged in 2001. The first accounts concerned a particularly notorious priest perpetrator and the way his case was handled in the archdiocese. Readers were horrified as they learned about Catholic leaders putting the rights of an adult above the need to protect children from harm. For most, these were the first stories they had ever heard about decisions of this nature. Sadly, in the world of child-serving organizations, they were not unique.

In June 2002 in Dallas, Tex., at their semi-annual meeting, the U.S. Conference of Catholic Bishops introduced the first truly comprehensive plan for preventing acquaintance abuse within a large-scale child-serving organization. It was not just a set of suggested policies. They and other organizations had made "suggestions" in the past. No, the Charter for the Protection of Children and Young People was a mandated blueprint for "large-scale organizational abuse prevention," which included education for multiple audiences, policy development, internal feedback systems, quality control, ongoing research and public accountability for following through with the plan. The implications of this plan, adopted by the largest child-serving organization in the United States, have proved more far-reaching than most Catholics realize.

With the issuing of the charter, the "industry standards" for child protection changed. Formerly unwritten rules, like not allowing a sexual offender to work with children and defining specific boundaries for ministry relationships, were now clearly articulated—not just for the Catholic Church, but for everyone. In August 2003 the Episcopal bishops in the United States issued their own national policy; requiring Episcopal child-and youth-serving organizations to have screening, monitoring, education, guidelines for interactions and plans for responding if someone reported concerns about abuse. Numerous churches, schools, camps and other child-serving organizations have implemented sexual-abuse prevention programs since 2002, both in response to the publicity of the Catholic sexual abuse cases and in response to the solutions that were defined as a result.

Sometimes people wonder when all this will be over. The truth is, coping with sexual abuse is part of all child-serving organizations. As long as we serve children and youth, we have no choice but to address sexual abuse and its prevention. We are growing in our understanding of sexual abuse and our appreciation of its complexity. Over time, perhaps we can begin to recognize the role we have played in bringing attention and concrete solutions to a problem that affects the lives of children throughout the world.

Am I still Catholic? Yes. I feel exceedingly proud of the work being done by so many to create and maintain parishes and schools where children do not have to be afraid. And while I pray we never forget our past, I am filled with hope for the future of our church and for the difference we can make in the lives of our children.

> "There are more uninsured children in Texas (1.24 million) than there are in 26 other states combined, including such large-population states as Oregon, Minnesota, Louisiana, Colorado, and Wisconsin."

Tax-Funded Programs Reduce Child Abuse and Neglect

US Newswire

This viewpoint, from US Newswire, provides an overview of the book Homeland Insecurity . . . American Children at Risk *by Michael R. Petit. The book examines how children are faring in each of the fifty states, comparing the top ten to the bottom ten in eleven areas, such as the percentage of children living past their first birthdays and the percentage of children living in poverty. Overall, children in so-called "blue" (Democrat majority) states are doing better than children living in "red" (Republican majority) states. According to the author of the book, this disparity is due to Democrats providing more social programs, which are made possible through higher taxes.*

As you read, consider the following questions:

1. How much more likely are the children in the bottom ten states to die before their first birthday as compared with children in the top ten states?

2. What state has the highest percentage of uninsured children in the nation?

3. How much would the "Homeland Insecurity" program cost?

Living in a "red" state appears to be more hazardous to the health of millions of American children, according to startling data contained in a major new book, *Homeland Insecurity . . . American Children at Risk.* . . . The factors weighed in the "Homeland Insecurity" ranking includes such diverse indicators as inadequate pre-natal care, lack of health care insurance coverage, early death, child abuse, hunger and teen incarceration.

Based on a diverse range of 11 child-related statistical measures, nine of the 10 top states with the best outcomes for children today are "blue" states (Wisconsin, Iowa, New Jersey, Washington, Minnesota, Nebraska, Massachusetts, Connecticut, Vermont and #1-ranked New Hampshire, with Iowa being the sole "red" state in the group) and all 10 of the bottom states with the worst outcomes for children are "red" states (Wyoming, Georgia, Arkansas, Alabama, South Carolina, Texas, Oklahoma, New Mexico, Louisiana and, in last place, Mississippi).

Republican vs. Democrat

The political dividing lines used in the book are "red" states (those that voted Republican in the 2004 presidential election) versus "blue" states (those that voted Democratic). *Homeland Insecurity . . . American Children at Risk* outlines a $500 billion "Invest in Kids" agenda to reverse the harmful impact of conservative ideology on children caused by the failure to invest in documented children's needs and by federal and state cuts in taxes and children's programs beginning in the early 1980s and accelerating since 2001.

More Taxes Lead to More Programs

Michael R. Petit, author of *Homeland Insecurity ... American Children at Risk*, and founder of Every Child Matters, said: "The bottom line here is that where a child lives can be a major factor in that youth's ability to survive and thrive in America. The reason why this is the case is no mystery: 'Blue' states tend to tax themselves at significantly higher levels, which makes it possible to reach more children and families with beneficial health, social and education programs. 'Red' states overwhelmingly are home to decades-long adherence to anti-government and anti-tax ideology that often runs directly contrary to the needs of healthy children and stable families."

Joel J. Alpert, MD, professor and chairman emeritus, Boston University School of Medicine, and past president, American Academy of Pediatrics, said: "It is unconscionable for policymakers and parents to allow two very different Americas to exist today for our children. Currently, millions of American children are without health insurance, millions are reported abused and neglected, millions are left unsupervised everyday after school, and millions have parents in a prison system that is crushing families. Many programs such as the State Child Heath Insurance Program and Head Start serve only a fraction of eligible children. We can and must erase the differences that exist today for children in 'red' and 'blue' states."

Life in the Bottom Ten

How serious is it for many children today in "red" states? The "red"/"blue" state dividing line is clear on issue after issue cited in *Homeland Insecurity*:

- A child in the bottom 10 states is twice as likely to die by the age of 14 as are children in the top 10. All 10 of the bottom states of this measure are "red" states. All of the top 10 states are "blue" states.

- Children in the bottom 10 states are 1.8 times as likely to be uninsured as children in the top 10. Nine of the 10 states in the bottom of this measure are "red" states. Eight of the top 10 states are "blue" states.

- Children in the bottom 10 states are seven times more likely to die from abuse and neglect as are children in the top states. Nine of the 10 bottom states of this measure are "red" states. Eight of the top 10 states are "blue" states.

- A child in a bottom-10 state is more than twice as likely to be living in poverty as a child in a top-10 states. All of the 10 states in the bottom are "red" states. Six of the top 10 states are "blue" states.

- Women in the bottom 10 states are more than twice as likely to receive inadequate prenatal care as women in the top 10 states. Eight of 10 states in the bottom of this measure are "red" states. Seven of the top 10 states are "blue" states.

- Juveniles in the bottom 10 states are almost two and a half times as likely to be incarcerated as juveniles in the top 10. Eight of the 10 bottom states of this measure are "red" states. Seven of the top 10 are "blue" states.

- Children in the bottom 10 states are 74 percent more likely to die before their first birthday as are children in the top 10. Eight of the 10 states in the bottom of this measure are "red" states. Seven of the top 10 states are "blue" states.

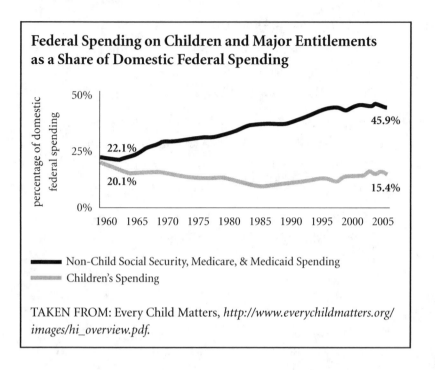

Federal Spending on Children and Major Entitlements as a Share of Domestic Federal Spending

percentage of domestic federal spending

50%

25%   22.1%

20.1%

0%

45.9%

15.4%

1960 1965 1970 1975 1980 1985 1990 1995 2000 2005

━━━ Non-Child Social Security, Medicare, & Medicaid Spending
▬▬▬ Children's Spending

TAKEN FROM: Every Child Matters, *http://www.everychildmatters.org/ images/hi_overview.pdf.*

The State of Texas

In order to illustrate the huge gap between "red" and "blue" states, the new book points to the serious circumstances facing more than a million children today in one of the crucibles of "compassionate conservatism": Texas. The Lone Star state has the highest percentage of uninsured children in the nation (24.6 percent v. 15.7 percent nationally), the fourth worst rate of immunizing two year-olds (75 percent v. 84 percent nationwide) and a teen birth rate that is 50 percent higher than the national average. There are more uninsured children in Texas (1.24 million) than there are in 26 other states combined, including such large-population states as Oregon, Minnesota, Louisiana, Colorado and Wisconsin. Texas also ranks #1 in both child abuse deaths and the percentage of households experiencing "food insecurity" (16.4 percent versus 11.4 percent nationwide).

Experts Agree

Sarah M. Greene, president and CEO, National Head Start Association, said: "I am pleased to see that the author correctly recognizes the danger posed to American children and, in fact, our nation in general by dwindling support for Head Start programs that target America's most at-risk children in order to get them ready to learn in school. We wholeheartedly endorse the portion of the 'Homeland Insecurity' that calls for full-scale national/state-level support for early childhood education . . . including full funding of Head Start."

Elizabeth J. Clark, PhD, ACSW, MPH, executive director, National Association of Social Workers, Washington, D.C., said: "The statistics that Mike Petit cites in 'Homeland Insecurity' are borne out in our work every day as social workers. Social workers are the women and men who are charged with working with children and their families in direct care and through national and state legislative advocacy. Social workers make an investment in our nation's children. We call on the government to make that same investment. Social workers are partners with educators and medical personnel to make positive changes in children's lives and we implore lawmakers to make their well-being the centerpiece of the 2008 elections and beyond."

The "Invest in Kids" Agenda

"Homeland Insecurity" outlines a 10-year, $500 billion "Invest in Kids" agenda to improve the life chances of all U.S. children, regardless of where they live. . . . Among the investments proposed:

Child Health. Create a universal children's health insurance program similar to Medicare for the elderly—Over 8,000,000 children do not have health insurance and millions more are at risk of losing their coverage. Combining and expanding Medicaid, S-CHIP, and employment-based insurance is achievable. The Every Child Matters Education Fund opposes any attempt by the Administration and Congress to cut or block-grant the Medicaid entitlement.

Child Abuse. Intensify federal efforts to reduce child abuse and neglect—Nearly three million reports of child abuse and neglect are made annually. Proven programs exist to prevent and treat child abuse, a widespread problem that contributes to many other social ills. The Every Child Matters Education Fund opposes any attempt by the Administration and Congress to block-grant the Title IV-E foster care program.

After-School Programs. Promote after-school programs that provide learning activities and connect the caring adults— After-school programs have been shown to help prevent crime, drug use, and teen pregnancy. Millions of unsupervised children and teens would benefit. The 21 Century Community Learning Centers program has not seen an increase in federal funding in three years, resulting in fewer and fewer children being served. The Every Child Matters Education Fund supports a substantial increase in funding for after-school programs.

Pre-School Education. Ensure that every child, regardless of income or background, has access to high quality pre-school education—Millions of eligible three and four year-olds are not enrolled in quality pre-kindergarten programs that can help prepare them for school. The Every Child Matters Education Fund opposes any effort by the Administration [and] Congress to block-grant or cut funding for Head Start and supports universal access to pre-school education for 3 and 4 year olds.

Working Families and Taxes. Extend the child tax credit to the working poor—Currently, families that make between $10,500 and $26,500 per year, even though they pay federal payroll taxes, do not receive the $1,000 per child credit that families with higher incomes receive. Extending tax cuts to these families will help lift them from poverty and simply show fairness as trillions of dollars in tax cuts have gone to more fortunate individuals.

> "Virtually all images of child pornography depict the actual sexual abuse of real children. In other words, each image literally documents a crime scene."

Law Enforcement Agencies and Child Advocacy Groups Can Stop Sex Predators by Working Together

U.S. Department of Justice

This viewpoint is from a prepared statement of U.S. Attorney General Alberto R. Gonzales regarding the sexual exploitation of children on the Internet. Speaking to the Senate Committee on Banking, Housing and Urban Affairs, Gonzales illustrates the shocking magnitude and severity of the crimes committed by child predators using the Internet, and he announces an initiative that brings together law enforcement agencies and nongovernmental organizations to combat this problem and make children safer.

"Prepared Gonzales Statement for Committee on Banking, Housing and Urban Affairs on Sexual Exploitation of Children on the Internet," September 19, 2006, http://www.usdoj.gov/archive/ag/testimony/2006/ag_speech_060919.html.

As you read, consider the following questions:

1. According to Alberto R. Gonzales, why is protecting children from sexual exploitation on the Internet a high priority for the U.S. Department of Justice?

2. According to a study by the University of New Hampshire for the National Center for Missing & Exploited Children, how many of all kids aged ten to seventeen who used the Internet were exposed to unwanted sexual material?

3. What are the three parts of the Project Safe Childhood initiative?

Mr. Chairman, Senator Sarbanes, and distinguished Members of the Committee, thank you for having me here today to discuss this vital issue of protecting our children from exploitation on the Internet.

As all of you know, none of us can under-estimate the importance, or the urgency, of this threat against our kids.

Every day, pedophiles troll the Internet to see and sell images of child abuse. They also look for ways to contact our children over the Internet. They are hoping to make contact with the very young, the very innocent, to commit unthinkable acts and potentially sell images of those crimes to other pedophiles.

It is unfortunate that one of the greatest inventions of our generation—the Internet—is providing a building ground for these heinous crimes. That is why parents, volunteers and law enforcement must make the Internet a battleground. We must fight every day because predators seek to hurt our kids every day.

As the father of two young boys, this issue is one that I take extremely seriously on both personal and professional levels. I know the same is true for members of this committee. We are all aware that a society's ability to protect its children is a critical marker of that society. That is why protecting our children from sexual exploitation on the Internet is a high priority of the Department of Justice.

The Horrific Truth

I know that the issue of child molestation, rape and pornography can be difficult for people to focus on because it is, simply, so terrible. But we cannot turn away to preserve our comfort level. We must confront the brutal facts. For example:

- Virtually all images of child pornography depict the actual sexual abuse of real children. In other words, each image literally documents a crime scene.

- These are not just "pornographic" pictures or videos. They are images of graphic sexual and physical abuse— rape, sodomy and forced oral sex—of innocent children, sometimes even babies.

- The Internet has created a shocking field of competition to see who can produce the most unthinkable photos or videos of rape and molestation. In the perverse eyes of pedophiles and predators, this means the younger, the better.

Working with federal investigators and advocacy groups, I have seen just how horrific these images can be. I have seen a young toddler tied up with towels, desperately crying in pain, while she is being brutally raped and sodomized by an adult man. I have seen videos of very young daughters forced to have intercourse and oral sex with their fathers and pictures of older men forcing naked young girls to have anal sex. These are shocking images that cry out for the strongest law enforcement response possible. Moreover, these disturbing images are only the beginning of a cycle of abuse. Once created, they become permanent records of the abuse they depict, and can haunt the victims literally forever once they are posted on the Internet. Unfortunately, advances in technology have also made it easier and easier for offenders both to profit from these images and to distribute them to each other. Once images are posted on the Internet, it becomes very difficult to remove them from circulation. Even more disturbing is the fact offenders rely on these images to develop a plan of action for targeting their next victims, and then use the images to groom victims into submission.

The challenge we face in cyberspace was illustrated by a new national survey, released in August 2006, conducted by University of New Hampshire researchers for the National Center for Missing & Exploited Children. The study revealed that a full third of all kids aged 10 to 17 who used the Internet were exposed to unwanted sexual material. Much of it was extremely graphic.

Project Safe Childhood

As I mentioned, this battle against child exploitation is a top priority. Earlier this year we launched a program called "Project Safe Childhood" that is helping to coordinate the good efforts of U.S. Attorneys offices, law enforcement and advocacy groups. Through Project Safe Childhood we are constantly expanding our efforts to address the sexual exploitation of children on the Internet and the financial underpinnings of this exploitation. The program is helping law enforcement and community leaders develop a coordinated strategy to prevent, investigate, and prosecute sexual predators, abusers, and pornographers who target our children.

As we've looked at ways to improve the law enforcement response to the problem of online exploitation and abuse of children, one thing we've continuously heard from state and local investigators and prosecutors is that many Internet Service Providers don't retain records for a sufficient period of time. Several months ago, I asked a working group within the Department to look at this issue, and we're working hard on ways to remedy this problem.

Project Safe Childhood Is Working

Under PSC [Project Safe Childhood], the number of federal child exploitation prosecutions has increased significantly, along with the number of federal, state, and local investigations and convictions, and more and more victims are being identified. PSC's education and awareness efforts complement this focus on enforcement.

- Enforcement:

- In U.S. Attorneys' Offices, 2,118 indictments were filed in fiscal year 2007 against 2,218 defendants. This represents a 27.8 percent increase over fiscal year 2006 (1,657 cases filed against 1,760 defendants).

- In fiscal year 2007, 332 child exploitation cases resulted in the forfeiture of 458 assets. The value of the forfeited assets is $5,237,490. This represents a 492.7 percent increase over fiscal year 2006.

- In fiscal year 2007, ICAC [Internet Crimes Against Children] Task Forces made 2,354 arrests for online child exploitation crimes across the nation, an increase of nearly 15 percent over the number of arrests in fiscal year 2006.

- At the end of calendar year 2005, 590 child pornography victims had been identified. . . . As of April 27, 2008 that number had grown to 1,342—an increase of more than 127 percent of the total in approximately two and a half years.

U.S. Department of Justice,
"Fact Sheet: Project Safe Childhood,"
May 7, 2008.

Working Together

I see the initiative to protect our children as a strong, three-legged stool: one leg is the federal contribution led by United States Attorneys around the country; another is state and local law enforcement, including the outstanding work of the Internet Crimes Against Children task forces funded by the Department's Office of Justice Programs; and the third is nongovernmental organizations, like the Financial Coalition Against Child Pornography and the National Center for Missing and Exploited Children—without which we would not have the Cybertipline.

I want to note that the Financial Coalition would not exist without the leadership and vision of the Chairman of this Committee, Senator Shelby, who was the catalyst in bringing industry leaders together to address this serious problem.

Congress has also provided invaluable support for our efforts by passing the Adam Walsh Child Protection and Safety Act of 2006. The Adam Walsh Act, signed by the President in July, will help us keep our children safe by preventing these crimes and by enhancing penalties for these crimes across the board.

None of our efforts can stand alone. All must involve high levels of sharing and coordination. That is what Project Safe Childhood is all about.

An International Issue

One final note that I'd like to share with the Committee today is that our fight against the proliferation of child sexual exploitation on the Internet does not stop at our borders. It demands a global strategy. This makes it imperative that we pay attention to the laws governing child sexual exploitation in other nations. Many countries have astonishingly lenient punishments for child pornography offenses. For instance, in several nations the production of child pornography is punished with only a fine or imprisonment of less than six months or a year. Simple possession is punishable merely by a fine. Just as we need some states to strengthen their laws to punish child sex offenders, we must encourage some foreign lawmakers to strengthen their laws as well, including those concerning the financial components of these crimes.

I am grateful that the Committee shares the Department's commitment to protecting our children. Again, I want to thank Chairman Shelby for establishing the Financial Coalition Against Child Pornography. I also want to thank Senator Santorum for authoring the provision in the Adam Walsh Act that authorized the Department's Project Safe Childhood initiative. Senators, your exemplary actions have truly shown the depth of your commitment to protecting our children from abuse that no human being should have to endure.

VIEWPOINT 6

"The first successfully prosecuted child-
abuse case did not occur until 1874—
and given the lack of a relevant statute,
had to be brought under laws prohibiting animal cruelty."

Striking a Balance Between Family Rights and State Intervention Is Difficult

Robert K. Vischer

*This viewpoint examines the history of the rights of the indi-
vidual within the framework of the family and the state. The
author discusses the United Nation's Convention on the Rights of
the Child, which seems to be a shift toward unprecedented rights
of children, including the right to investigate other religions and
ways of life before deciding to follow the paths of their parents.
The author also takes a closer look at the trend toward child autonomy, calling for caution. Robert K. Vischer teaches at the St.
Thomas School of Law in St. Paul, Minnesota.*

Robert K. Vischer, "All in the Family," *Commonweal*, vol. 134, March 23, 2007, pp. 8–9.
Copyright © 2007 Commonweal Publishing Co., Inc. Reproduced by permission of
Commonweal Foundation.

As you read, consider the following questions:

1. According to Robert K. Vischer, what reason did U.S. delegates give for not ratifying the Convention on the Rights of the Child?

2. What one question sums up the tension created by the children's rights movement?

3. What does Vischer say that child's rights advocates believe is the proof of adequate parenting?

When is it proper for the state to intervene in a family on behalf of a child's well-being? Most Americans agree that the state can, and should, remove a child from physically abusive parents. What about parents who relentlessly mock the sexual orientation of their son? Or teach their daughter that women should never work outside the home? Or forbid their child's exposure to any "secular" books, music, or art?

A refuge of intimacy and tenderness in a world frequently lacking both, the family has traditionally been shielded from state intrusion that, in deference to parental authority, still shapes American law. And yet every day headlines recount another heartbreaking story of a family that has served not as a refuge from suffering, but as the source of it.

Individual Liberty

The debate over the state's role in regulating the family reflects a broader movement in the law's treatment of the individual. Nearly one hundred fifty years ago, the English jurist and historian Sir Henry Maine famously summed up the history of law in Western society as a progression "from status to contract." While past eras defined individuals according to group membership, modern law began recasting individuals as autonomous beings, free to arrange their affairs as they see fit. For all his foresight, Maine may not have imagined the extent to which our current law would pursue individual liberty. Today we ensure that individuals are not excluded from jobs or housing based on their race, ethnicity, or gender. We have begun to ensure that pharmacists and other health-care professionals are not required to perform services that conflict with their moral convictions. We even ensure that women are not diverted from the kind of life they've chosen by an unwanted pregnancy.

Liberty and the Family

The family is not exempt from our legal system's pursuit of greater individual liberty. A generation ago, the ability of individuals to abandon unhappy marriages expanded vastly through the creation of the no-fault divorce. More recently, defining a man and woman as fixed elements of marriage has come under fire as an unfair limitation on the freedom of same-sex couples to order their family structures as they choose. The last frontier for liberty's march within the family is the parent-child relationship. Until the late nineteenth century, the legal system treated children wholly as the property of parents, even in cases of extreme abuse and neglect. The first successfully prosecuted child-abuse case did not occur until 1874—and given the lack of a relevant statute, had to be brought under laws prohibiting animal cruelty. Today, as our myriad social-service agencies attest, the public's willingness to interfere with a family on behalf of children has expanded dramatically.

It is clear that state intervention in cases of physical abuse or neglect—even to the point of removing a vulnerable child from her family—has alleviated a great deal of suffering. But broken bones and bruises aren't the only harms that preclude a child's flourishing. Parents who abuse a child verbally, fail to provide adequate schooling, forbid meaningful interaction with peers, teach self-hatred, or foreclose opportunities to explore the world outside the family are unmistakable threats to the child's growth. Should society intervene in such cases? Traditionally, the notion that the state should act to protect a child's holistic development has been a nonstarter. But many influential children's rights advocates have begun to link a broader view of a child's well-being to a more robust framework of proposed rights. Whether their efforts will bear fruit in our legal system remains to be seen.

Convention on the Rights of the Child

One manifestation of this shift was the effort in the United Nations in the late 1980s and in the '90s to establish a global framework of children's rights. Its Convention on the Rights of the Child requires signatory nations to ensure that children enjoy freedom of expression, thought, conscience, religion, a right to privacy, and the ability to "receive information and ideas of all kinds." The United States remains one of only two nations (the other is Somalia) not to ratify the convention. The U.S. delegation argued that the convention's enforcement would erode parental control over child rearing. Whether or not those fears are well-founded, the convention's terms mark an important reconception of the child's legal significance. And as the focus broadens from ensuring the child's physical well-being to ensuring that she develops the ability to choose her own life path, the grounds for state intervention could expand exponentially. That expansion creates a new set of problems.

Parents Or the State?

Lacking a fully developed rational capacity, children are incapable of protecting their own interests or directing their own lives. Someone must make decisions on their behalf. Who should that be? Except in cases of extreme abuse or neglect, the law has traditionally deferred to the parent. This deference was not a grant of permission, but a recognition of a relationship that precedes and transcends state authority. As children's rights advocates succeed in persuading the state to oversee progression from childhood to full autonomy, the state's atti-

Convention on the Rights of the Child

Since its adoption in 1989 after more than 60 years of advocacy, the United Nations Convention on the Rights of the Child has been ratified more quickly and by more governments (all except Somalia and the United States) than any other human rights instrument. This Convention is also the only international human rights treaty that expressly gives non-governmental organisations (NGOs) a role in monitoring its implementation. . . .

The basic premise of the Convention is that children (all human beings below the age of 18) are born with fundamental freedoms and the inherent rights of all human beings. Many governments have enacted legislation, created mechanisms and put into place a range of creative measures to ensure the protection and realisation of the rights of those under the age of 18. Each government must also report back on children's rights in their country.

Child Rights Information Network,
"Convention on the Rights of the Child,"
2008, www.crin.org.

tude toward parents becomes much less deferential. By asserting authority to ensure a child's healthy development, the state also claims authority to define what healthy development is. The UN has provided one set of criteria. But once the authority has shifted from parents to the state, the vision's content is open to public debate.

For instance, the focus on the child's future exercise of autonomy has led some children's rights advocates to call for more aggressive regulation of private schools. One common objective is to ensure that a school's teaching promotes essential values such as equality and tolerance. University of Chicago law professor Emily Buss goes even further, asserting that "a state interest in fostering the capacity for independent thought in its children could justify policies encouraging and even, perhaps, compelling some amount of exposure to ideologically unlike peers." In other words, the state has an interest not just in regulating the content of the curriculum, but also in regulating the makeup of the classroom.

The State as Guardian

Such assertions of state interest may make it more difficult for parents to raise their children within a religious tradition that seeks to separate itself from society, such as the Amish, or one holding unpopular views, whether on the status of women or the morality of homosexual behavior. Family law scholar James Dwyer writes that if "some parents cannot use their children's schooling to proclaim the 'good news,' because in the state's judgment the parents' news is not so good, then so be it." Dwyer's new book, *The Relationship Rights of Children*, takes the principle of individual autonomy to its logical conclusion within the family. Portraying the parent-child relationship as a straightforward creation of the law, Dwyer asserts, "the state directly determines who a child's legal parents will be at the time of birth and then at every moment of a person's childhood."

Unlike political theorists who call for the state to mold children into model citizens, Dwyer invokes state power on behalf of the child's own well-being, urging the state to "respect any measure of autonomy [children] already possess and [to] optimize their development toward full autonomy." And yet even such benign-sounding prescriptions pose problems. Who will decide what optimizes that development toward autonomy? Because the child cannot articulate her own well-being, Dwyer's policy guideline actually elevates the state, as the child's guardian, over the parent.

Individual Autonomy

Of course, no one longs for a return to the days when child abuse was a strictly private affair. But there are reasons to worry about a reform that would allow the state to implement a value—individual autonomy—that is not of absolute importance to many parents who love their children dearly. For example, many political theorists insist that for a person to direct her own life as a truly "autonomous" being, she must be able to evaluate critically the tradition into which she was born before deciding to live within that tradition as an adult. Their claim is not that a "cradle Catholic" cannot be an autonomous adult and remain Catholic, but that she must take stock of the merits and drawbacks of her own tradition, as well as alternative worldviews, before deciding to remain Catholic. Needless to say, creating space for this critical reflection is hardly a pressing concern for most parents—and indeed, many may reject it. And therein lies the crux. It is one thing to disagree with one's fellow parents about the centrality of individual autonomy as an objective of child rearing; it is quite another for the state to choose sides.

Who Is Most Trustworthy?

Ultimately, the tension created by the children's rights movement is captured in a single question: Whom do we trust to care for the child? Once the state assumes the authority to speak for a child what happens if the parents fall into a category of people—for example, drug abusers, prisoners, the mentally incompetent—who tend not to act in a way that is most supportive of a child's future autonomy? Under Dwyer's prescription, these parents would bear the burden of proving their worth before the state permitted them to act as parents. It is not difficult to imagine future calls to expand the category of those presumed to be unfit parents to include individuals who would threaten their child's autonomy by passing on misogynist or homophobic religious beliefs. When parenthood exists as a creation of the state, the boundaries of state power become difficult to discern.

The state must tread lightly and cautiously whenever it seeks to enlarge its regulatory presence within the family, even when its motivation is noble and its aims laudatory. We cherish the family because it is the social foundation of human experience—the community where the human person loves most deeply, sacrifices most nobly, and relates most authentically. It is much more than a mere training ground for the future exercise of autonomy, and its value is not readily captured in the language of public norms and legal rights. We would do well to recall the perspective of Catholic social teaching, as expressed in chapter 5 of the *Compendium of the Social Doctrine of the Church*: "The family," it reminds us, "does not exist for society or the state, but society and the state exist for the family."

The pleas of children's rights advocates cannot be dismissed lightly, nor can they be answered by retreating to the archaic notion of the child as parental property. For those who care deeply about the well-being of children but resist the enshrinement of autonomy as the proof of adequate parenting, the task is to discern when a family's failure to function as a refuge of love and care justifies the corrective exercise of state power. Blurring the boundaries between the family and the state may in certain cases produce better outcomes for some children, but it also threatens the independence that makes the family such a vital component of the child's flourishing. How do we carve out a role for the state in guarding the inherent dignity of the child without turning parents into licensed state agents? This is the hard question, and we'll have to answer it soon.

Periodical Bibliography

The following articles have been selected to supplement the diverse views presented in this chapter.

Mitru Ciarlante   "Disclosing Sexual Victimization," *The Prevention Researcher*, vol. 14, no. 2, April 2007, pp. 11–14.

Marianne K. Dove and Kenneth L. Miller   "Child Sexual Abuse: What Every Educator Should Know," *The Delta Kappa Gamma Bulletin*, Spring 2007.

Education Week   "States Weigh Plans to Address Educator Sexual Abuse," vol. 27, no. 22, February 6, 2008, p. 16.

Michael Friscolanti   "A National Embarrassment," *Maclean's*, vol. 121, no. 1, January 14, 2008, pp. 46–53.

Jane Gross   "Lack of Supervision Noted in Deaths of Home-Schooled," *The New York Times*, January 12, 2008.

Gregory A. Hession   "This Is Child Protection?" *The New American*, July 23, 2007, pp. 14–18.

Home School Legal Defense Association   "Tragedy Prompts Calls for Heightened Scrutiny of Homeschoolers," February 5, 2008. www.hslda.org/hs/state/dc/200802050.asp.

Richard G. Jones and Corey Kilgannon   "After 3 Die, Questions on Why Erratic Mother Kept Custody," *The New York Times*, February 26, 2008.

Tara McKelvey   "No Parent Left Behind," *American Prospect*, vol. 18, no. 12, December 2007, pp. A13–A14.

US Newswire   "Child Abuse and Neglect Cost Nation Over $100 Billion per Year; Most Federal Child Welfare Funds Unavailable for Prevention Services and Supports," January 29, 2008.

For Further Discussion

Chapter 1: What Constitutes Child Abuse?

1. In light of the discussion of prenatal care, poverty, parental drug use, religion, sibling relationships, and the use or non-use of corporal punishment, does society's interest in child rearing inform and direct life in the home? Should it?

2. In her article criticizing California's proposed ban on parental spanking, Debra Saunders writes, "Parents are not stupid, they know the difference between beating and spanking." Apart from the extremes, is there a "gray area" where distinguishing between the two might not be so easy?

3. In his article, Richard Dawkins states that the religious instruction/indoctrination of children should be considered a form of child abuse. His argument focuses on Christianity and Roman Catholicism in particular. Does his argument hold up with other expressions of Christianity? With other religions (such as Islam, Buddhism, Hinduism)? Might an expanded consideration of other religions strengthen or weaken his argument?

Chapter 2: What Causes Child Abuse?

1. While Brian W. Clowes and David L. Sonnier make the case for a strong connection between homosexuality and pedophilia, Joe Kort argues that homosexuals are no more likely to molest children than any other segment of the population. In both viewpoints the authors specifically state that this argument should be decided by objectively examining empirical, scientific evidence. Does either article do a better job of meeting this criteria?

2. Paul J. Fink's viewpoint on military deployment and child abuse highlights the correlations between increased family stress and an increase in abuse. How might family stress impact the reporting or under-reporting of abuse by other family members or the abuse victims themselves? Consider, also, Jill King Greenwood's viewpoint on live-in boyfriends and child abuse? Why might the mothers be reluctant to speak up about abuse?

3. Lesli A. Maxwell's viewpoint on educators using technology as a means to sexually abuse students raises the issue of "appropriate" contact between teachers and students. Which uses of technology do you see as appropriate? Where should the lines be drawn with regard to e-mail, cell phone contact, texting, and social networking sites?

Chapter 3: How Does Child Abuse Affect Its Victims?

1. How does the discussion of the studies of rat pups and stress in "Abuse May Disrupt Brain Development in Children" connect with the strategies for recovering from abuse trauma cited in Victoria L. Banyard and Linda M. Williams' viewpoint?

2. In "Unreleased Emotions from Child Abuse Can Create Devastating Anger," what do you think Dr. Neher should say to Mr. Kelley upon reentering the examining room?

Chapter 4: How Can Child Abuse Be Prevented?

1. In the viewpoint "Tax-Funded Programs Reduce Child Abuse and Neglect," the writer observes a correlation between child abuse and states' status as a "red state." Do you find this argument compelling? What other issues—other than "red state" status—might account for higher abuse issues in those states?

2. The author of "Striking a Balance Between Family Rights and State Intervention Is Difficult," reminds readers of the Catholic understanding of the role of the state in family matters when it says, "The family does not exist for society or the state, but society and the state exist for the family." In Robert K. Vischer's opinion, the "United Nation's Convention on the Rights of the Child" argues that the opposite is true. Which view is right? Who is truly responsible for the welfare of children?

Organizations to Contact

The editors have compiled the following list of organizations concerned with the issues debated in this book. The descriptions are derived from materials provided by the organizations. All have publications or information available for interested readers. The list was compiled on the date of publication of the present volume; the information provided here may change. Readers need to remember that many organizations take several weeks or longer to respond to inquiries.

ACT for Kids
210 West Sprague Ave., Spokane, WA   99201
(866) 348-KIDS (5437) • fax: (509) 747-0609
e-mail: resources@actforkids.org
Web site: www.actforkids.org

ACT for Kids, a program of Lutheran Services Northwest, provides resources, consultation, research, and training for the prevention and treatment of child abuse and sexual violence. Resources for the deaf community, the Hispanic community, as well as the English speaking community include workbooks, manuals, brochures, games, videos, and books—including titles such as *My Very Own Book About Me* and *How to Survive the Sexual Abuse of Your Child.*

American Professional Society of the Abuse of Children (APSAC)
350 Poplar Ave., Elmhurst, IL   60126
(877) 402-7722 • fax: (630) 359-4274
e-mail: apsac@apsac.org
Web site: www.apsac.org

The APSAC is dedicated to improving the coordination of services in the fields of child abuse prevention, treatment, and research. It publishes a quarterly newsletter, the *Advisor*, as well as the *Child Maltreatment Journal.*

Association of Sites Advocating Child Protection (ASACP)
5042 Wilshire Blvd., #540, Los Angeles, CA   90036-4305
(323) 908-7864
e-mail: comments@ascap.org
Web site: www.asacp.org

ASACP is a nonprofit organization dedicated to eliminating child pornography from the Internet. ASACP battles child pornography through its reporting hotline and by organizing the efforts of the online adult industry to combat child sexual abuse.

Center for Effective Discipline, Inc. (CED)
155 West Main St., Suite 1603, Columbus, OH   43215
(614) 221-8829 • fax: (614) 221-2110
e-mail: Info@StopHitting.org
Web site: www.stophitting.org

The CED provides educational information to the public on the effects of corporal punishment of children and alternatives to its use. It is the headquarters for and coordinates both the National Coalition to Abolish Corporal Punishment in Schools (NCACPS) and End Physical Punishment of Children (EPOCH-USA). The center publishes current news stories, legal information, suggestions for parents, and links to research on its Web site.

Child Welfare League of America (CWLA)
2345 Crystal Drive, Suite 250, Arlington, VA   22202
(703) 412-2400 • fax: (703) 412-2401
Web site: www.cwla.org

CWLA is an association of nearly 800 public and private non-profit agencies that provide a range of services to more than 3.5 million abused and neglected children and their families each year. In addition to publishing research and information on its Web site, CWLA publishes *Children's Voice*, a quarterly magazine, and *Child Welfare*, a bi-monthly journal.

Childhelp USA

15757 North Seventy-eight Street, Scottsdale, AZ   85260
Hotline: (480) 922-8212
Web site: www.childhelpusa.org

Childhelp USA is dedicated to helping victims of child abuse and neglect. The organization operates a hotline that victims can call twenty-four-hours-a-day to speak with professional counselors. Childhelp USA also operates treatment facilities and regional centers that provide services to abused children.

Family Research Laboratory (FRL)

126 Horton Science Center
University of New Hampshire
Durham, NH   03824-3586
(603) 862-1888 • fax: (603) 862-1122
e-mail: doreen.cole@unh.edu
Web site: www.unh.ed/frl

The FRL is an independent research group that studies the causes and consequences of family violence, including physical and sexual abuse of children, and the connections between family violence and other social problems. A bibliography of works on these subjects, produced by staff members under the sponsorship of the University of New Hampshire, is available from the FRL.

Klaas Kids Foundation

PO Box 925, Sausalito, CA   94966
(415) 331-6867 • fax: (415) 331-5633
e-mail: klaaskids@pacbbell.net
Web site: www.klaaskids.org

The Klaas Kids Foundation was established in 1994 after the kidnapping and murder of twelve-year-old Polly Hannah Klaas. The foundation's goals are to acknowledge that crimes against children deserve a high priority and to form partnerships with concerned citizens, the private sector, organizations, law enforcement, and legislators to fight crimes against children. The foundation publishes a quarterly newsletter, the *Klaas Action Review*.

National Center for Missing and Exploited Children (NCMEC)
699 Prince St., Alexandria, VA   22314
(800) THE LOST/1-800-843-5678
Web site: www.missingkids.com

The NCMEC serves as a clearinghouse of information on missing and exploited children and coordinates child protection efforts with the private sector. A number of publications on these issues are available, including guidelines for parents whose children are testifying in court, help for abused children, and booklets such as *Child Molesters: A Behavioral Analysis* and *Child Pornography: It's a Crime*.

Rape, Abuse & Incest National Network (RAINN)
2000 L Street NW, Suite 406, Washington, DC   20036
(202) 544-3046 • fax: (202) 544-3556
e-mail: info@rainn.org
Web site: www.rainn.org

RAINN is the nation's largest anti-sexual assault organization. RAINN operates the National Sexual Assault Hotline and carries out programs to prevent sexual assaults, help victims, and ensure that rapists are brought to justice. Its Web site contains statistics, counseling resources, prevention tips, news, and more.

Safer Society Foundation
PO Box 340, Brandon, VT   05733-0340
(802) 247-3132 • fax: (802) 247-4233
Web site: www.safersociety.org

The Safer Society Foundation is a national research, advocacy, and referral center for the prevention of sexual abuse of children and adults. The Safer Society Press publishes studies and books on treatment for sexual abuse victims and offenders and on the prevention of sexual abuse, including *Fuel on the Fire: An Inquiry into "Pornography" and Sexual Aggression in a Free Society*.

Bibliography of Books

Robin E. Clark, Judith Freeman Clark, and Christine A. Adamec

The Encyclopedia of Child Abuse. New York: Facts On File, 2007.

Kenneth N. Condrell

The Unhappy Child: What Every Parent Needs to Know. Amherst, NY: Prometheus Books, 2006.

Cynthia Crosson-Tower

Understanding Child Abuse and Neglect. Boston: Pearson/A&B, 2005.

Lynne Curry

The DeShaney Case: Child Abuse, Family Rights, and the Dilemma of State Intervention. Lawrence, KS: University Press of Kansas, 2007.

Julia C. Davidson

Child Sexual Abuse: Media Representations and Government Reactions. Milton Park, Abingdon, England: Routledge-Cavendish, 2008.

Joseph E. Davis

Accounts of Innocence: Sexual Abuse, Trauma, and the Self. Chicago: University of Chicago Press, 2005.

William L. Fibkins

Innocence Denied: A Guide to Preventing Sexual Misconduct by Teachers and Coaches. Lanham, MD: Rowman & Littlefield Education, 2006.

David Finkelhor   *Childhood Victimization: Violence, Crime and Abuse in the Lives of Young People.* New York: Oxford University Press, 2008.

Mary Gail Frawley-O'Dea   *Perversion of Power: Sexual Abuse in the Catholic Church.* Nashville: Vanderbilt University Press, 2007.

Richard B. Gartner   *Beyond Betrayal: Taking Charge of Your Life After Boyhood Sexual Abuse.* Hoboken, NJ: John Wiley & Sons, 2005.

Sherri Mabry Gordon   *Beyond Bruises: The Truth About Teens and Abuse.* Berkeley Heights, NJ: Enslow, 2009.

John Haley and Wendy Stein   *The Truth About Abuse.* New York: Facts On File, 2005.

Marci Hamilton   *Justice Denied: What America Must Do to Protect Its Children.* Cambridge, England: Cambridge University Press, 2008.

Chris Hansen   *To Catch a Predator: Protecting Your Kids from Online Enemies Already in Your Home.* New York: Dutton, 2007.

Denise A. Hines and Kathleen Mailey-Morrison   *Family Violence in the United States: Defining, Understanding, and Combating Abuse.* Thousand Oaks, CA: Sage Publications, 2005.

Karen L. Kinnear   *Childhood Sexual Abuse: A Reference Handbook.* Santa Barbara, CA: ABC-CLIO, 2007.

Linda J. Koenig   *From Child Sexual Abuse to Adult Sexual Risk: Trauma, Revictimization, and Intervention.* Washington, DC: American Psychological Association, 2004.

Steven Levenkron and Abby Levenkron   *Stolen Tomorrows: Understanding and Treating Women's Childhood Sexual Abuse.* New York: W.W. Norton, 2007.

Donileen R. Loseke, Richard J. Gelles, and Mary M. Cavanaugh   *Current Controversies on Family Violence.* Thousand Oaks, CA: Sage Publications, 2005.

Gerald P. Mallon and Peg McCartt Hess   *Child Welfare for the Twenty-First Century: A Handbook of Practices, Policies, and Programs.* New York: Columbia University Press, 2005.

Dave Pelzer   *Help Yourself for Teens: Real-Life Advice for Real-Life Challenges Facing Young Adults.* London: Michael Joseph, 2005.

Jodi A. Quas and Jeffrey J. Haugaard   *Childhood Sexual Assault Victims: Long-Term Outcomes after Testifying in Criminal Court.* Boston: Blackwell Publishing, 2005.

Edward L. Rowan   *Understanding Child Sexual Abuse.* Jackson, MS: University of Mississippi Press, 2006.

Pamela D. Schultz   *Not Monsters: Analyzing the Stories of Child Molesters.* Lanham, MD: Rowman & Littlefield, 2005.

Julian Sher   *Caught in the Web: Inside the Police*
                     Hunt to Rescue Children from Online
                     Predators. New York: Caroll & Graf,
                     2007.

Index

A

Abuse
depression factors in, 36, 137, 162
emotional, 67, 71, 135, 179
federal efforts against, 208
mental *vs.* physical, 36, 38
online, 96
poverty as, 66–67, 71–72
psychiatric disorders from, 131–135
shaken baby syndrome, 189
sibling bullying as, 57–58, 59
state intervention in, 219
threatening behavior as, 153–155
See also Assault; Corporal punishment; Domestic violence; Sexual abuse; Spanking

Abusers
acquaintances as, 195
"ephebophiles" as, 111, 113
"pederasty," 114–115
potential, 189–190
statistics on, 72
See also Catholic Church; Homosexual men; Juvenile abusers; Pedophiles

"Acquaintance abuse," 195

Acquired immunodeficiency syndrome (AIDS), 145, 149

Acute stress disorder (ASD), 88

Adam Walsh Child Protection and Safety Act, 215, 216

Add Health study (National Longitudinal Study of Adolescent Health), 146

Adrenocorticotropic hormone (ACTH), 130

Advocacy group issues
child's rights, 218, 220–221, 224
coordinated services, 141
custody battles, 14–16
homosexuality, 118
law enforcement agencies and, 210–216
parental drug use, 50–52
religious indoctrination, 42
social worker legislation, 207
See also Corporal punishment

After-school programs, 208

Aggression in children, 24, 56–58, 62, 137, 190

Alcoholism, 45, 46, 56, 117

Alpert, Joel J., 204

Alvy, Kerby, 21–27

American Psychiatric Association (APA), 115

Anger issues
indications, 152–153
misdirected, 153
physiological responses, 130
shaken baby syndrome, 189
threatening behavior, 153–155
uncovering, 155

Applewhite, Monica, 193–201

Archives of Sexual Behavior (journal), 110–111